BEFORE ROSWELL

The Secret History of UFOs

Ken Goudsward &
Barbara M. DeLong

ISBN: 978-1-989940-58-7

dimensionfold.com

We would like to thank Mark Eddy for introducing us to one another. He is a good man with a remarkable talent for connecting people. We could not have written this book without him.

Introduction

The famous Roswell incident is, in the perspective of many, the origin of what we have come to know as the UFO phenomenon, or in recent times, "the UAP threat". Roswell was indeed a major turning point in terms of public awareness as well as government involvement, at least in the USA. But it didn't start at Roswell. The aim of this book is to show that the public view of UFOs beginning in 1947 is merely a continuation of longstanding phenomenological patterns. Our focus will be on the abundance of historical UFO sightings from before Roswell, working back through the centuries into antiquity and beyond. As Barbara sums up, "No anomalous phenomena is as enduring through the ages, more witnessed and reported, or more discussed and debated than the UFO phenomenon." From as early as 1639 in this country when Governor John Winthrop of the Massachusetts Bay Colony reported accounts in his diary to the Niaux Caves of France dated 10,000 BC to 13,000 BC. UFO's have been an enduring aspect of the mysteries of life as we know it within our environment.

Modern UFO phenomena tend to occur in a variety of flavors, but this variety is by no means infinite. In fact, there are really only a handful of differences that crop up when examining the testimonies of UFO witnesses and ET experiencers. These phenomena are remarkably repeatable. We will attempt to identify patterns within the evidence, as well as historic changes within these patterns.

Nowadays in the USA, between four thousand and six thousand sightings are reported each year. Thousands more are reported all around the world and there have been many documented UFO cases from Canada, all over Europe, Africa, Asia, South America, and Australia.

UFOs do not come in all shapes and sizes. There are a very limited set of configurations that are widely reported around the world:

- Saucers
- Triangles and V-shapes
- Ovals and "Tic-Tacs"
- Long rods or pillars or "cigars"
- Large looming shapes with lots of lights
- Orbs

UFOs Throughout History

1947 - Roswell, New Mexico: The celebrated Roswell crash in July 1947 is the most famous case of flying saucers, as well as government mismanagement and cover-up. Many versions of the story may differ slightly in details, but many parts remain constant. A UFO crashed on a ranch just outside of Roswell, alien bodies were discovered, and the news sources reported that the government had captured a flying saucer. The next day, the military issued a report denying the claims and stating that the debris recovered was from a weather balloon. However, the weather balloon explanation is a clear fabrication, as evidenced by the further top-secret communications and special projects which ensued. A letter dated 23 September 1947 from Lt. Gen. Nathan F. Twining, Chief of Staff of the U. S. Army to the Commanding General of the Army Air Force establishing an official study of flying saucers to be called *Project Sign*. The setting up of Project Sign evidently took too long in the eyes of top brass, so it was escalated in priority in a letter dated 30 December 1947 from Maj. Gen. L. C. Craigie. The army demanded action, and it demanded it in a hurry. Obviously they were under no illusions that weather balloons proved such an imminent threat.

June 24 1947 - Mount Rainier, Washington: Two weeks before the Roswell story broke, Kenneth Arnold was on an aerial search for a crashed C-46 marine transport plane when he saw 9 objects flying in formation. He estimated their speed at 1,300 to 1,700 miles per hour, distance at 23 miles and length of formation to be 5 miles. Also in the air at the time was a DC-4, which Arnold used as a point of reference to estimate the size of individual discs. He estimated the size as two-thirds the size of the DC-4. This sighting attracted significant media attention and public interest.

1947 - White Sands, New Mexico: C. J. Zohn stationed at White Sands proving grounds in New Mexico watched a huge, silver, circular disc at a height of 10,000 feet above the installation. This sighting was just days after Kenneth Arnold's sighting.

1947 - Bisbee, Arizona: John A. Petsche, electrical worker and another witness independently saw a disk-shaped object, which seemed to land near Tintown.

1947 - Douglas, Arizona: Mrs. Coral E. Lorenzen watched a light rise from across the Mexican border, assume a spherical shape and disappear among the stars on June 10. The sighting lasted 10 seconds. Mrs. Lorenzen and her husband, Jim, subsequently founded the Aerial Phenomena Research Organization.

1947 - Grand Canyon, Arizona: A Navy lieutenant was flying at 9000 m toward the south, near Williams Field, when he saw two circular objects diving at "unconceivable" speed. They were gray, about 3 m in diameter, and appeared to land 40 km south of the Grand Canyon.

1947 - Edwards Air Force Base, Muroc, California: Four witnesses: 1st Lt. Joseph McHenry, T/Sgt Ruvolo, S/Sgt Nauman, and Miss Janette Scotte watched for an unstated length of time while two disc-shaped or spherical objects, silver and apparently metallic, flew a wide circular pattern, and then one of them later flew a tighter circle, moving about 300 mph at approximately 8,000 feet." More officers gathered as a third object came into sight. A test pilot had reported seeing a round object at about 12,000 feet the day before.

1947 - Manitou Springs, Colorado: A silvery object was seen approaching from the northwest toward Manitou Springs on May 19. It halted, remained motionless for some minutes, and then started performing complex aerobatics. It rose and flew out of sight, against the wind.

1947 - Emmett, Idaho: Captain E.J. Smith, pilot of United Airlines Flight 105, plane encountered five flying discs over Emmett on July 4.

1947 - Twin Falls, Idaho: Two boys and their father saw a sky-blue object in the Smoke River Canyon 100 m away and 25 m above ground. Treetops under it were spinning wildly, although the object itself did not spin. It made a swishing sound. Shape: inverted plate, 7 m diameter and 3.5 m thick. There was a red flame on one side of the top.

1947 - Lake Mead, Nevada: While cruising at 6,000 feet, US Air force pilot Lieutenant Armstrong witnessed six discs flying in formation.

1947 - Fargo, North Dakota: Lt. George F. Gorman of the North Dakota National Guard was piloting an F-51 fighter jet, on approach to Fargo. The tower called his attention to a Piper Cub which he saw below him. As he prepared to land, suddenly what he took to be the tail-light of another plane passed him on his right, but the control tower assured him no other planes were in the area. Chasing the light, he got within 1,000 yd. of it. It had been blinking but suddenly became steady and started to move rapidly with the F-51 in pursuit. There followed a complicated chase in which Gorman had to dive on one occasion to avoid collision. Suddenly the light began to climb and disappeared. The Air Weather Service provided an official analysis in which the incident was explained as a balloon.

1947 - Yukon, Oklahoma: A salesman reported seeing six strange objects in the sky at dusk. 'They appeared as large as washtubs, and were very high up, flying in formation and at an incredible speed.'

1947 - Portland, Oregon: Newspapers ran a report with a photo generating much excitement. This picture was later claimed to be a weather balloon.

1947 - Houston, Texas: Eastern Airlines DC-3, pilot Clarence S. Chiles and co-pilot John B. Whitted, were on a regular run from Houston to Atlanta, At 2:45 a.m. they saw a bright light dead ahead coming rapidly toward them. They pulled to the left to avoid a collision. Looking back they saw the UFO go into a steep climb. The pilots described it as a wingless B-29 fuselage and said that the underside had a deep blue glow.

1947 - Richmond, Virginia: Meteorologist Walter A. Miczewski and his staff at the US Weather Bureau in Richmond, Virginia, were tracking a weather balloon with a theodolite. They then noticed a silver disk, flat bottomed, with a dome on top, crossing the sky from east to west. The object was larger than the balloon and was tracked for about 15 seconds before it was lost to view.

May 18 1947 - Richmond, Virginia: Several observers saw a flat, white, cigar-shaped object speed across the sky at sunset, heading north-west.

May 5 1947 - Washington: A silvery object was reported to have fallen out of the sky and disintegrated over Washington state.

July 5 1947 - St. Maries, Washington: Eight flying saucers were reported landing on a mountainside in full view of ten witnesses.

1947 - Spokane, Washington: Eight disk-shaped objects the size of a house, were seen flying at 1000 km/h. A civilian woman stated that the objects fell with a dead leaf motion and landed before ten witnesses on the shore of the Saint Joe River, in Idaho.

1947 - Tacoma, Washington: Harold A. Dahl and others allegedly saw six tire-shaped objects, 30 m in diameter, metallic with dark openings, over Puget Sound near Maury Island. One of the objects exploded, showering the witnesses with metal.

Oct. 14 1947 - 11 miles. NNE of Cave Creek, Arizona. Noon MDT. Witnesses: ex-AAF fighter pilot J.L. Clark, civilian pilot Anderson, third man. Watched 45-60 seconds while one 3-foot "flying wing"-shaped object, which looked black against the white clouds and red against the blue sky, flew straight at an estimated 380 m.p.h., at 8-10,000 feet, from NW to SE.

July 6 1947 - Fairfield-Suisan Air Base, California. Daytime. Witnesses: Army Air Forces Capt. and Mrs. James Burniston. Watched for 1 minute while one object having no wings or tail rolled from side-to-side three times and then flew away very fast to the southeast.

July 29 1947 - Hamilton Air Base, California. 2:50 p.m. PDT. Witnesses: Assistant Base Operations Officer Capt. William Rhyerd, ex-AAF B-29 pilot Ward Stewart. Watched for unknown length of time while two round, shiny, white objects with estimated 15-25 foot diameters, flew 3-4 times the apparent speed of a P-80, also in sight. One object flew straight and level; the other weaved from side-to-side like an escort fighter.

July 9 1947 - Meridian, Idaho. 12:17 p.m. PDT. Witness: Idaho statesman aviation editor and former (AAF) B-29 pilot Dave Johnson. Watched for more than 10 seconds from an Idaho Air National Guard AT-6 while a black disc, which stood out against the clouds, made a half-roll and then a stair-step climb.

July 3 1947 - Harborside, Maine. 2:30 p.m. EDT. Witness: astronomer John Cole of South Brooksville, Maine. Watched 10-15 seconds while ten very light objects, with two dark forms to their left, moved like a swarm of bees to the northwest. A loud roar was heard.

Sept. 3 1947 - Oswego, Oregon. 12:15 p.m. PDT. Witness: housewife Mrs. Raymond Dupui. Watched for unknown length of time as 12-15 round, silver objects flew an unstated pattern.

Oct. 11 1947 - Dodgeville, Wisconsin. unnamed civilian man. Watched for 1 hour while an undescribed object flew counterclockwise circles.

1947 - Maillardville, British Columbia, Canada: Residents witnessed flashing discs streaking through the sky at noon-time on Sunday. Antoine Beauregard, painter, said he was working on a house during the afternoon and suddenly saw a shiny aluminum disc cross the sky. It was about 300 feet long.

July 10, 1947 - Harmon Field, Newfoundland, Canada. Between 3 and 5 p.m. local time. Witnesses: three ground crewmen, including Mr. Leidy, for Pan American Airways. Watched briefly while one translucent disc- or wheel-shaped object flew very fast, leaving a dark blue trail and then ascended and cut a path through the clouds.

1947 - Bauru, Brazil: A group of survey workers ran away as they heard a hissing noise and saw a disk land 50 m away. Jose C. Higgins saw two figures through a window. Later three beings in shiny clothes and translucent suits, with oversized bald heads, huge round eyes, no eyelashes or eyebrows, and a metal box on their back, emerged from the craft. They were over 2 m. tall. They drew the solar system and pointed to Uranus as if to suggest that was their point of origin.

1947 - Hungary: According to the files of the USAF's Aerospace Technical Intelligence Center, some 50 reports were made across Hungary of 'silvery balls' flying at great speed in the daylight.

1947 - Raveo, Italy: An Italian artist by the name of Rapuzzi Johannis was taking a leisurely walk in the mountains between Italy and Yugoslavia. He saw a red glowing saucer on the ground just in front of him, about thirty feet in diameter. The ship was accompanied by two small men with very large heads with greenish faces, lacking eyebrows, but with a circle around each eye. Their hands had eight talon-like fingers. They wore helmets and dark blue coveralls with red collars and belts.
One of the creatures hit Johannis with an electrical discharge weapon, leaving him very weak and almost

paralyzed. After incapacitating him, the creatures ignored Johannis and eventually departed.

***

Thirty-three UFO sightings have been documented and survived the historic record from 1947. Most of the sightings occurred in the western USA, west of the Rocky Mountains. In fifteen of the cases, objects seen were disc or saucer shaped, six were spheres, and three were cigar shaped. Nine of these cases involved multiple UFOs, ranging from five to twelve in number. Two of the ships crashed. Five cases appear to be indicative of some type of cloaking technology used on the craft. In nine of the cases the witnesses were impressed by the speed and maneuverability of the craft. Three of the incidents included observation of entities outside their ship. In one case the entities injured the witness.

1946 - Sweden: In the eight-month period from May to December of 1946, close to two thousand UFO sightings were reported. Around ten percent were tracked on radar. Most of the objects were cigar-shapes, though a few discs and spheres were reported. Many of them disappeared into lakes. The so-called "Ghost Rocket" invasion of Sweden was well documented, and official investigations took place involving Scandinavian, British, and U.S. military authorities. A number of "ghost rocket" sightings also took place in Greece, Italy, Portugal, and Belgium.

1946 – Antarctica: In August 1946, the United States Navy sent a fleet of 13 ships, 33 aircraft, and 4,700 men to occupy Antarctica under the leadership of Admiral Richard E. Byrd. Ostensibly, the mission, named "Operation Highjump" was for scientific research, which seems like a highly dubious priority for the navy amidst the aftermath and ongoing fortifications following World War II.

By the time the top-secret mission was called off ahead of schedule in February 1947, Admiral Byrd himself admitted publicly that the mission was in fact no research mission, but that the fleet had been sent ready for combat and did in fact engage in arial combat against an enemy with vastly superior flight technology.

Byrd warned the press that "the United States should adopt measures of protection against the possibility of an invasion of the country by hostile planes coming from the polar regions" and that "the United States could be attacked by planes flying over one or both poles" and "that the time has ended when we were able to take refuge in our isolation and rely on the certainty that the distances, the oceans, and the poles were a guarantee of safety."

Aside from these verified quotes, much speculation, rumor, and possible misinformation has surrounded Operation Highjump, such that it has become difficult to determine which "facts" may or may not be true, with some pundits writing off the entire operation as a myth, and others adding a great many more details, some of which are most likely fraudulent. In the opinion of these authors, Operation Highjump was a real mission that did take place, and did include aerial combat between the United States Navy and flying craft of an unidentified nature, however, the details of the encounters have become too obfuscated to comment upon.

1946 - Tampa, Florida: Pilot and crew of a C-47 aircraft 30 miles north-east of Tampa, saw a large cigar-shaped object with luminous portholes hurtle towards them in horizontal flight at the same altitude of 4,000 ft. At 1,000 yards distant it swerved to avoid them. Estimated size of object was "twice that of a B-29 bomber", or two hundred feet long.

1945 - Wonsan, North Korea: Three Japanese "Zero" fighter planes engage two discs in a dogfight. One plane is shot down, and the UFOs flee into space.

1945 - Aleutian Islands, Alaska: Fourteen men on the USAT Delarof saw a dark spherical object rise out of the water, circle their ship and fly off to the south.

1944 - Klagenfurt, Austria: Major Leet, a bomber pilot, saw a luminous disc follow his plane and its maneuvers.

Dec. 22, 1944 - Hagenau, Germany: Lt. David McFalls of the U.S. 415th night fighter squadron was over Hagenau, Germany. At 6:00 am, he saw two "huge, bright orange lights" climbing toward the plane. McFalls dived, banked and turned his plane, but the UFOs stuck with him for two minutes, then peeled off and blinked out.

August 10, 1944 - Palembang, Sumatra: Captain Alvah M. Reida was piloting a B-29 bomber based at Kharagapur, India, on a mission over Palembang, Sumatra, when his right gunner and co-pilot noticed a sphere 'probably five or six feet in diameter, of a very bright and intense red or orange in color' that constantly throbbed, about 12,500 ft off the starboard wing. It kept up with the B-29, then flying at 210 mph. Reida tried to shake it off his plane, but it stayed in the same relative position until , after eight minutes, it 'made an abrupt 90 degree turn and accelerated rapidly, disappearing in the overcast.'

February 22, 1944 - Washington, DC: Franklin D. Roosevelt wrote a Top Secret memo on White House stationary for "The special committee on non-terrestrial science and technology." Both the title and the content clearly allude to extraterrestrial life, the former using the word "non-terrestrial" and the latter talks about "coming to grips with the reality that our planet is not the only one harboring intelligent life in the universe."

1943 - Burma: US bomber pilots flying missions from Burma to China reported being buzzed and circled by ‘glittering’ objects. Instruments failed to operate until the objects flew off.

1943 - Qing Xian, China: A domed UFO that emitted a white light was seen flying less than 20 feet above the ground.

October 14, 1943 - Schweinfurt, Germany: U.S. B-17s of the 348th Bomb Group had started a bombing run over Schweinfurt, Germany, when they ran into a formation of ‘scores’ of small, silvery disks, about one inch thick and four inches in diameter, flying toward the bombers. Major E.R.T. Holmes reported that one struck the tail of one aircraft, but without effect.

1943 - Pushkino, Russia: Soldiers saw a disc-shaped object hovering very high in the air, apparently above aircraft level.

1942 - Japan: An Imperial Japanese “Sally” bomber aircraft, on a mission over the Sea of Japan, was approached by a small dark spherical object which flew around and between the aircraft in the formation. An alert gun-cameraman snapped one photograph.

1942 - Solomon Islands: While in the Solomon Islands US Marine Corp Sgt. Stephen J. Brickner sighted a staggering number of UFOs, laid out in virtually an enormous rectangle. They were in rows of 15 objects long by ten objects deep. The formation was 15 craft long and 10 deep. Formation sightings have been reported before but the rectangle shape is unique.

1942 - Timor Sea: The Dutch cruiser Tromp was approached by a large aluminum disc that flew at tremendous speed. It then circled the vessel for about three to four hours. Finally, it flew off at an estimated speed of 3,000-3,500 mph.

February 24 1942 - Los Angeles, California: A gigantic black-out, covering the area from Bakersfield south to San Diego and eastward to Boulder City and Las Vegas, Nevada, went into effect shortly after 8 PM on orders from the Army Fourth Interceptor Command. It continued until 11:03 p.m. As Los Angeles went dark amongst considerable confusion and uncertainty, The Interceptor Command announced, "this is not a practice black-out." A yellow signal, indicating the approach of enemy air raiders, was flashed on the state-wide teletype at 7:35p.m.. Police said the signal indicated the presence of unidentified airplanes approaching Los Angeles from the sea but did not necessarily mean they were enemy. Anti-aircraft and machine gunners scrambled to their weapons at Ft. Mac Arthur, which was promptly placed on alert basis. Reports that the sound of gunfire could be heard could not be verified from listening posts at the beach or at the harbor. Definite indication that the Interceptor Command meant business by calling for the black-out was contained in a statement from a spokesman who said: "There are planes over the south of Los Angeles that are unidentified. The area will be blacked out until we can identify them." When asked if Army planes had been sent aloft to contact these aircraft the spokesman said: "You can assume there have been." Thousands of residents, listening with straining ears for sounds of aircraft, were unable to distinguish sounds of motors, however. A few minutes after the black-out was ordered, the flashing of what appeared to be Army searchlights was visible in the higher portions of Los Angeles, 25 miles from the waterfront. Headquarters of the Fourth Interceptor Command, calling the blackout a success, said they had a report that unidentified planes were in the vicinity of Los Angeles. The following day swarms of children combed the beaches collecting pieces of shrapnel that littered the beach which the local military rewarded them with small compensations. All of that which was collected were determined to be from our military. Eyewitnesses reported that it seemed that our munitions exploded before they hit the targeted objects. There was some collateral damage, all of which was determined to be from our weapons.

1941 - Germany: German aviatrix Hannah Reisch sees a UFO speeding by at an altitude of 66,000 feet.

1941 - Cape Giradeau, Missouri: Charlotte Mann states her grandfather, Rev. Wm. Huffman, told her about a UFO crash site story which occurred in July 1941 outside of Cape Giradeau. The Cape Giradeau police department and some military personnel were at what they thought was a plane crash site, but Rev. Hoffman said it obviously was not a plane. There was crumpled aluminum like metal debris scattered over the area and an object that was disc shaped. There were three humanoid bodies, child-like with large heads, big black eyes, no nose, slit for a mouth, and a form fitting uniform covered with debris. The MJ-12 cited this Missouri Ozarks 1941 UFO crash site story along with the

Roswell 1947 crash sites as recovered exhibits deemed extraterrestrial.

1940 - Bata, Hungary: A “fiery cartwheel” UFO is seen ascending from a hilltop in Bata, Hungary. This sighting is particularly notable for its uniqueness with similarities to UFO descriptions common over two thousand years prior.

1940 - Japan: While flying over Japan, Wing Commander D.J. Blakeslee sighted an object he described as having red, green and white lights. The craft moved rapidly to escape detection but was tracked by ground radar. The Air Force officially claimed the sighting to be Jupiter.

Throughout World War II, hundreds of pilots on both sides of the conflict reported, “Foo fighters,” bright, unidentified flying objects that move in the sky in a strange manner. Often described as either swarms of red or green luminous balls or groups of small metallic disks, they followed aircraft or flew around them, giving the impression of intelligent behavior. Some observers saw them touch the wings or the tail assemblies of the aircraft without causing any visible damage, thus raising the question of whether they were material objects at all. Numerous other sightings concerning larger, cigar-shaped, disk-shaped, or sphere-shaped objects were also recorded in both camps. Authorities on both sides of the war took these reports seriously and treated them as a threat, both sides initially assuming them to be secret enemy weaponry or reconnaissance of some kind.

***

The encounters during the war years and immediately following, can be divided roughly into two groups. Cigar shaped objects in Europe in 1946, and spheroidal or saucer/disc shaped objects prior to 1946 and spanning the globe. There were reports of instrument failure aboard at least one witness vehicle, and one plane was even shot down by a UFO. It should be noted in this case, it was the witnesses who engaged the UFOs into combat maneuvers. A wide range of sizes were reported during this period, ranging from a few inches to two hundred feet in diameter. Some of the craft appear to have been amphibious, either emerging or disappearing into the water.

The Thirties

1938 - Tabor, Saskatchewan, Canada: "Mysterious lights" hover over the countryside and are seen on multiple occasions over a week period in early December.

1938 - Juminda, Estonia: Two observers watched a 1-meter-long object that was greenish -brown in color until it finally disappeared.

1938 - USA: While not an actual UFO encounter, The Orson Welles' Radio Broadcast of H. G. Wells' novel, "War of the Worlds", is worthy of inclusion here due to its effect on the public reception of UFOs conceptually. It was the first widely publicized story of interplanetary warfare involving Earth. Before his story, previous tales described peaceful beings visiting Earth, but Wells' aliens came with weapons and were ready to take over the Earth as their new home. These aliens, who came from Mars, had so much power that humans could not stand a chance against them (although in the end a type of bacteria finally kills the aliens). As a direct result of this novel, people began to believe that any alien invasion would mean the termination of mankind. Orson Welles with his Mercury Theatre on the Air broadcasted their version of Wells' novel on Halloween night, 1938. It began at 8 p.m., and even before the broadcast was through, millions of people were frightened to the point that they cried, prayed, tried to rescue loved ones, and called upon ambulances and police. There was nationwide panic like never before. The people perceived this play as being reality because at the time radio was their most reliable source of news, and everything was portrayed so realistically. Also, some of the specific places described, for example, street names, were real for many people. From this intense reaction, we can conclude that at this time in history, our culture believed that extraterrestrial life exists, and that aliens are capable of traveling to Earth by UFO's to invade our planet.

1936 - Guipuzcoa, Spain: A sighting in the midst of the Spanish Civil War. English novelist and former soldier Valentine Williams and two others were driving from General Franco's headquarters in Burgos to Biarritz, France. The sighting occurred at 4:18 pm in the Basque province of Guipuzcoa, about 75 miles from San Sebastian. Williams' companions gasped in amazement; he turned to see what he thought was a flare or traced round on a course at right angles to the road, heading northward at an amazing velocity. Williams later described it as 'like a streamer of white smoke... As it went, it burst into a bright orange flame. There was no sound or explosion.' When they reached Biarritz, they told their story. Tom Dupree, from the British Consulate at Hendaye, said he had been at San Sebastian (about 30 miles west of Biarritz) at the same time of that day and had seen the same object. This UFO could have been a particularly large fireball, burning brightly enough to be visible by daylight. However, the accounts give the impression that the object was traveling parallel to the ground, not falling towards the earth.

1935 - Nipawin, Saskatchewan, Canada: Three witnesses saw a landed UFO at Nipawin and watched several little entities in silver suits ascending and descending a ladder. Square imprints and burnt areas seen and photographed at the location the next day.

1935 - Addis Ababa, Ethiopia: During the Ethiopian War a disc-shaped object hovered motionless in the sky above and was seen by many witnesses.

1934 New York City: During a winter blizzard, mysterious engine noises are heard above the clouds.

1933 - Nambour, Queensland, Australia: A small disc hovers behind a house in Nambour, It is grabbed by a boy, who suffers itching and blistering on his hands as a result of grabbing the object.

1933 - Scandinavia: The month of December saw the beginning of the Swedish 'Ghost Flier' Wave. It ended four years later with an accumulation of 1,000 reports that also covered neighboring Finland and Norway. Most sightings involved airplane-shaped craft and luminous phenomena, none identified.

1933 - Chrysville, Pennsylvania: A man observed a faint violet light in a field between this town and Morrestown. Walking to it, he found an ovoid object 3 m in diameter and 2 m thick with a circular opening similar to a vault door. Pushing it, he found the room full of violet light and observed many instruments, no occupant. Smell of ammonia.

1932 - St. Paris, Ohio: A picture of George Sutton taken near midday shows an unidentified flying object over Sutton's left shoulder in this photograph. A vintage automobile with a 1932 license plate on the front bumper is in the photo. Nobody has been able to account for the dark object seen in this picture. It could not have been a street lamp, simply because there were no street lamps there at that time. There are no power poles or power lines visible anywhere in this picture.

1931 - Tasman Sea: Sir Francis Chichester was on a flight across the Tasman Sea when what looked like a dull gray-white airship approached him. It was pearl-shaped, flashing brightly, periodically vanishing, re-appearing, accelerating and finally disappeared.

1930 Mandurah, Western Australia. A small humanoid alien shows up at a farm in Mandurah, asking for water. It is shot to death by a terrified farmer.

***

The thirties included a higher than average percentage of close encounters of the second and third kind, resulting in burnt ground, blistered hands, along with some radiation poisoning on a witness, and the death of an extraterrestrial by human hands.

The Twenties

1929 - Ferme-Neuve, Quebec, Canada: Twenty-year-old Levis Brosseau, was returning home when he saw a dark object with a yellow light and his horse became very nervous. Within 6 m of the object four or five dwarfish figures were running back and forth. He heard their pointed, childlike voices, then saw the dark object take off with a machinelike sound and a rush of air. Estimated size of object: 15 m diameter, 5 m high.

1929 - Robsart, Saskatchewan, Canada: Five persons among them Einar Rostivold, saw a huge ball of light giving off fiery colors, 25 km from Robsart. It landed slowly, vanished gradually after illuminating the whole countryside for 30 min.

1929 - North Atlantic: Thomas Stuart, third mate of the SS Coldwater, reported that at 400 miles off the coast of Virginia he saw a light traveling at an estimated 100 mph toward Bermuda. 'There was something that gave the impression that it was a large, passenger craft,' he said, though investigation failed to show any airship or airplane on that course at that time.

1927 - Romania: A cylindrical object flew over a Rumanian village at an altitude of 200-300 m from west to east. Smoke gray in color it was an estimated 15-20 m in length and had a diameter of 3-4 m. It was not illuminated and passed soundlessly.

1927 - Sausalito, California: Writer Ella Young said that while sitting outside the Madrona Hotel she saw 'a cigar shaped craft shoot out of a cloud beyond the bay, and across the sky toward Tamalpais.' It was not shaped like any airship she knew. 'It was long and slender, of yellow color, and traveling at great speed… it seemed to progress by alternately contracting and elongating its body.'

1927 - Scottsbluff, Nebraska: While flying near Scottsbluff, pilot Barney Oldfield finds his biplane flanked by "flying manhole covers."

1926 - China: Nicholas Roerich sees a daylight disc UFO in a clear blue sky in northern China.

1926 - Mongolia: During his expedition explorer Nicholas Roerich and members of his caravan, caught sight of a huge oval-shaped object high in the sky. It had a shiny surface that reflected the sun on one side and moved at great speed north to south.

1925 - Chevy Chase, Maryland: Mysterious fireball explodes just outside Chevy Chase.

1925 - Moora, Australia: Two teenagers stumbled upon a saucer-shaped shimmering object resting on four legs in a paddock near. They ran off in fear.

1924 - County Wexford, Ireland: Two boys watched for several minutes as a solid beam of light several feet long traveled through the air a few feet from the ground. It moved at approximately 10mph, climbing a hedge and

crossing a field, before encountering a railroad t
moving off along its length.

1923 - Quetta, Pakistan: A UFO explodes in mid-air over Quetta. Flaming debris rains down, destroying a few buildings. The fire lasts for hours, leaving only melted slag and “thin wires.”

1922 - Poland: Many witnesses in observe a silvery object, two hemispheres divided by a rotating ring. The object ‘shoots’ a beam of light, and then rises with a loud noise.

1922 - Davenport, Iowa: Twin girls aged 8 see a daylight disc UFO near Davenport.

1922 - Hubbell, Nebraska: William C. Lamb was following strange tracks when he heard a high-pitched sound and saw a circular object intercepting starlight. It became brilliantly lighted and landed in a hollow. Soon afterward, a creature over 2.4 m tall was seen flying from the direction where the object had landed. It left tracks in the snow, which Lamb followed without results.

1922 - Barmouth, Wales: John Morris and William James saw an object fall into the ocean so slowly that it was thought to be a plane. A boat was sent out, but nothing was found.

1921 - Killingly, Connecticut: Bright circular UFOs seen above a cloud overcast at night.

1920 - Mount Pleasant, Iowa: Fishermen see a blue egg-shaped UFO touch down near Mount Pleasant.

***

In the twenties, both short and tall entities were seen associated with discs and spherical ships. Strange motion was observed, including an apparently undulating craft, and a small object that was observed to follow ground contours and patterns including railroad tracks.

The Early Twentieth Century

1919 - Wiltshire, England: Two British soldiers see several orange spherical UFOs hovering over Salisbury

1918 - Lismore, Australia: Luminous cruciform UFO seen hovering over Lismore, N.S.W., Australia.

1918 - Waco, Texas: Edwin Bauhan was one of several soldiers at Rich Field in Waco Texas who observed a 100 to 150 foot long cigar-shaped object after leaving the mess hall. "It came directly overhead and was no more than five hundred feet high so we got an excellent view of it. It had no motors, no rigging, it was noiseless, a rose or sort of flame color, I could observe no windows. We all experienced the weirdest feeling of our lives and sat in our tent puzzling over it for some time."

1917 - Belgium: The flamboyant fighter pilot Baron Manfred von Richtofen, known as "the Red Baron" not only shot down 80 enemy planes for the Germans during World War I, he also was the first human in history to gun down an alien spaceship! That's the fascinating claim of former German Air Force ace Peter Waitzrik, who says he watched in astonishment as the deadeye fighter pilot shot a UFO with undulating orange lights out of the sky over Belgium in 1917. Then, Waitzrik says, he stared in disbelief as two bruised and battered occupants of the downed craft climbed from their spaceship and scampered off into the woods — apparently never to be seen again. "The Baron and I gave a full report on the incident back at headquarters and they told us not to ever mention it again," the feisty,

105-year-old retired airline pilot recently told a reporter. "And except for my wife and grandkids, I never told a soul. But it's been over 80 years, so what difference could it possibly make now?" The aging Waitzrik said he and Baron Manfred von Richtofen — the renowned Red Baron — were flying an early morning mission over western Belgium in the spring of 1917 when the UFO suddenly appeared in a clear, blue sky directly ahead of their Fokker triplanes. "We were terrified because we'd never seen anything like it before," recalled the easygoing great-great grandfather of five. "The U.S. had just entered the war, so we assumed it was something they'd sent up. "The Baron immediately opened fire and the thing went down like a rock, shearing off tree limbs as it crashed in the woods. Then the two little baldheaded guys climbed out and ran away." Waitzrik said he assumed the glittering silver spaceship was some sort of enemy invention until the flying saucer scare that began in the late 1940s convinced him that his buddy had shot down a UFO. "The thing was maybe 40 meters (136 feet) in diameter and looked just like those saucer- shaped spaceships that everybody's been seeing for the last 50 years," the awed oldster said. "So there's no doubt in my mind now that that was no U.S. reconnaissance plane the Baron shot down, that was some kind of spacecraft from another planet and those little guys who ran off into the woods weren't Americans, they were space aliens of some kind."

1917 - Fatima, Portugal: Such phenomena include disks, like an "aircraft of light," described exactly in these terms by the witnesses of the fifth apparition. Also observed were double supersonic detonations, light protuberances, electrostatic charges, and moving "stars," mysterious white flowers or snow that dropped down from the "aircraft of light," but disappeared when it made contact with the ground. These descriptions of "snow" or mysterious white "flowers" are quite similar to the descriptions of "angel hair" that are well known from some famous UFO cases. This was accompanied by additional unexplained aerial phenomena, in the form of glowing spheres and disc-shaped objects. A UFO sighting had taken place before a crowd of somewhere between 50,000 – 100,000 people! The story given was that a silver disc appeared just as "the rain stopped and the clouds rolled back, the sun dimmed out and everything took on a gray, opaque appearance". The disc then dove in an erratic, zigzag pattern at the crowd, stopped just above their heads and then slowly maneuvered back into the sky. As it faded from view, the sun brightened and began to shine again normally. A local reporter took a photo of the disc.

1917 - Salida, Colorado: Minister and family use a telescope to watch a silver UFO shaped like a wagon wheel.

1916 - Undisclosed location in Europe: "A zeppelin-like object rose straight towards the clouds in the rear of our lines not like a flying machine, but straight up. After running vertically, it suddenly darted forward at a pace which must have been 200 m.p.h. It then turned around and darted backwards and then suddenly rising, disappeared in the clouds." Maurice Philip Tuteur, a soldier on the British front during WWI, in a letter to his parents. The object was also allegedly witnessed by two sergeant majors.

1916 - Svalbard Island, Norway: Fishermen working nets north of the island see a "dark Zeppelin" moving quickly over the Arctic pack ice, heading for the North Pole.

1916 - Ballinasloe, Ireland: A bright object was seen hovering in the sky. It was visible for fifteen minutes before traveling to the northwest. It was then observed to hover for a further forty-five minutes. It eventually vanished for good after Venus rose on the horizon.

1915 - Ottawa, Ontario, Canada: Numerous mystery aircraft were witnessed over the capital city of Ottawa. The event was reported in newspapers as the Phantom Invasion of Canada.

1915 - Gallipoli, Turkey: During battle in World War I, a regiment of the British Army, "the 1st 4th Norfolk", disappeared in an attempt to take Hill 60 at Suvla Bay near Gallipoli. In front of 22 witnesses, the regiment, over 800 men strong, marched into a strange fog formation of lenticular clouds hovering over Hill 60 and was never seen again. Posted as missing, the regiment was thought to have been captured. After the war, Britain demanded the return of the regiment, but the Turks denied any knowledge of the regiment's existence. No trace of the regiment has ever been found.

1914 - Georgian Bay, Ontario, Canada: Eight witnesses saw a UFO floating on the water of Georgian Bay. Entities were manipulating a hose dipped into the water. On seeing the witnesses they returned inside, all except one who was still outside when the craft took off.

1914 - Alta, Norway: On the evening of September 17, from 9 to 10 o'clock, a strange and so far unexplained luminous phenomenon was observed by many people and from many quarters. The sky was completely overcast and it was full dark when a luminous point like a very large star appeared to the east over Elvebakken, proceeded over Bosekop, disappeared behind Skoddevarre, came out again at Kvaenvik and after several other movements disappeared in the direction of Talvik. The light was white as a rule but shifted in part over to red and blue. It was also observed by binoculars from the small steamboat 'Sina'. Naturally it was guessed to be from an airplane. The light moved at various heights and as a rule without particularly great speed, except when it disappeared."

1914 - Solum, Norway: An airship was seen here at 8 o'clock yesterday morning December 20. Many reliable people, among them the sheriff of Solum, sighted the airship. The sheriff watched it with binoculars. It was at a dizzying height and moved first inland, but then turned southward and went away to sea.

1914 - Tjolta, Norway: At Midlandet in Tjolta last Saturday evening November 21, an airship was seen again cruising about Skjaervaer Lighthouse, which it lighted up with a searchlight. The airship, which had a height of about 700 meters, descended to about 400 meters altitude, wherefrom it let the searchlight play on a passing ship. Thereafter it ascended again. Between 20 and 30 people watched it simultaneously.

1914 - Benton Harbor, Michigan: Three luminous UFOs fly low over.

1913 - Toronto, Ontario, Canada: Several office workers watched what they concluded to be a fleet of airships passing west to east in groups. They then returned later in a scattered formation. No airships or airplanes were ever identified with this report.

1913 - England: Reports of multiple multi-colored lights, often accompanied by a powerful searchlight.

1913 - Lansing, Michigan: From the Lansing State Journal, June 30, "So swiftly did the strange craft travel that it was not more than three minutes until it had passed from sight in the northwest. The aerial mystery carried no lights of any description and was too elongated for an ordinary balloon. The craft was at a great height and when it passed to the northwest of the city had reached a still higher altitude." A sizeable crowd at a racetrack in Lansing Michigan witnessed the event.

1913 - Wisconsin: Large cigar-shaped UFO flies slowly over Milwaukee and Sheboygan, Wisconsin, flashing its bright spotlight over streets and buildings, and then retreats back out into Lake Michigan.

1912 - Chisbury, Wiltshire, England: Charles Tilden Smith reported the following case to the respected British science journal, "*Nature*". For over half an hour Smith observed two fan shaped or triangular 'heavy shadows' cast onto clouds overhead. The clouds were moving rapidly, but the shadows remained stationary in the sky. From time to time the unidentified apparitions varied in size. Smith concluded that two large unseen objects in the west were intercepting the Sun's rays.

1912 - Kent, England: Mysterious airships hover over cities and towns in Kent.

1912 - Lockport, Illinois: Witnesses watched, as an object appeared to traverse the moon's face for about three minutes. It was rectangular with absolutely flat ends, about two-thirds the diameter of the full moon in length.

1911 - New York: "Mystery airship" flies under the Brooklyn Bridge in New York City.

1910 - France: A photograph of entry number 5 in the Catalan Cup Race at a track in France. This picture also included a strange unidentified flying object seen over the treetops beyond the line of spectators watching this race. There is no indication whether the photographer saw this object and intended to get it in the picture.

1910 - Invercargill, New Zealand: Several witnesses, among them the vicar, the mayor, and a policeman, saw a cigar-shaped object hovering at 30 m altitude. A man appeared at a lateral door and was heard shouting some words in an unknown language. The opening closed, and the object accelerated and was lost to sight.

1910 - Normandy, France: The crew of a French fishing boat operating off the coast saw ‘a large, black, bird-like object’ fall from the sky into the sea, then bounded back before it fell once more and disappeared under the waves.

1910 - Alabama: Large cigar-shaped UFO hovers over Huntsville, Alabama and Chattanooga, Tennessee, playing its bright spotlight over both cities.

1910 - Fulton County, Arkansas: Myrtle B. Lee reported an experience she had with her brother when they were children in Fulton County Arkansas, “We saw a bright object hovering just above the trees about 50 yards from us. It was silver colored and shaped like a Zeppelin, but not quite as big. It had nothing hanging from the underside and there were no windows. When it took off we saw it start up, and it completely vanished before our eyes. We called it a balloon. When I saw a real balloon, I knew what Jack and I saw wasn’t a balloon. No one believed us when we told of seeing this thing.”

***

Note. Zeppelins were first flown commercially in 1910 by Deutsche Luftschiffahrts-AG (DELAG), the world's first commercial airline, based in Germany. Their first zeppelin was completed in June and first flown on 19 June 1910. Its maximum cruising speed was 32 mph. However, these early zeppelins were limited to Europe, as transatlantic flight did not become possible until 1928.

***

1909 - Donghoi, Vietnam: An elongated object following a west to east trajectory flew over the town. It gave off a strong light and was seen by two fishermen to plunge into the sea 6 km away from the coast, after a steady flight of about 9 min.

1909 - Peterborough, Cambridgeshire, England: The first mystery airship – or 'scareship', as it has since become known – was seen in Peterborough, Cambridgeshire, by two police officers in different parts of the city, at 5:10 am on March 23rd. A long oblong body with a light attached passed overhead at speed, making 'the steady buzz of a high power engine.' After a six-week long investigation, a Peterborough police spokesman claimed that the officers had seen an illuminated kite.

Throughout the year, many more mystery airships were seen almost exclusively at night, across many parts of Britain. Most were described as oblong in shape and equipped with a large searchlight, the crafts was capable of propelling itself through the air at great speed.

1909 - Caerphilly, Wales: Mr. Lethbridge was walking along a road near the mountains when he saw on the grass a large tubelike machine. Aboard were two men wearing furs and talking excitedly in a language the witness could not understand. The grass was found depressed at the site after the object had flown off.

1909 - Persian Gulf: Objects described as rotating wheels which could go under water were sighted and a Danish captain.

1909 - Worcester, Massachusetts: Witnesses reported rays proceeding from a lamp about the size of the searchlight of an automobile. As it came nearer it was apparent that the lamp was attached to a large black object, but the machine was so high that its form could not be distinguished. The object circled around Worcester, moved west to Marlborough where it was also observed and then returned to Worcester where it hovered for a time over an insurance building before leaving the area.

1909 - New Zealand: A rash of UFO sightings were reported in New Zealand in July 1909.

On July 19, three residents of Oamaru, reported “a flickering light” moving about in the sky.

On July 23, a group of schoolchildren and other residents of Kelso reported that an airship came down and bobbed around in the sky over the school for a few minutes.

On July 24, a group of boys playing on the beach at Kaka Point saw a huge, illuminated object moving about in the air. It appeared as if it was going to alight at Kaka Point. The light from it was distinctly reflected on the roof of Mr. Fitzgerald’s cottage. The boys thought it was being attracted by their lantern and left it on the beach. The airship then glided around the rocks at the old pilot station and nearly came in contact with them. It shortly afterwards disappeared. The boys said it was as big as a house.

The following night July 25, the mysterious object again made its appearance at the beach and was seen by Mr. George Smith and Mr. Poulter about 8:30 PM. Mr. Smith viewed it through a very powerful night glass. It was apparently over Mr. Aitkenhead's house when he first saw it, but it glided high in the air and sailed north in the direction of Kaitangata, swooping west and east and finally disappearing over the horizon. About 10:30 Mr. Smith was called out by Mr. Poulter to see the airship, which again had made its appearance. This time it headed out to sea and eventually disappeared. As seen through the glass, Mr. Smith said it appeared to be a fair size, dark superstructure with a powerful headlight and two smaller lights at the side.

On July 27, about 10 a.m., Mr. Allan Mitchell and Mr. Alex Riach, while working at Lambourne near the mouth of the Pomehaka River, saw high in the air a large boat-shaped structure floating in the air.

On July 28, a UFO came down over the city of Dunedin. A resident in the North Eastern Valley reported that he was awakened by a horrible noise at about 2:00 AM. "The noise was like a ship dragging her anchor up or a windlass of a steamer with dry-gear wheels working. I got up and went round to the front and I saw something floating up past Knox College. It was a great black thing with a searchlight attached.'"

On July 31, there was a UFO incident during the early morning hours at Greenvale, near Gore, South Island. While feeding the horses, a Greenvale farmhand heard a strange whirring sound, which frightened the animals. On looking out, he saw an airship overhead about 150 feet long. It had head and taillights and was moving so fast that, when he woke up his mates, the lights were faint in the distance.

At 4:55 PM, July 31, an Akatore resident witnessed a dark object shoot over the brow of the hills in the east and rapidly climb towards the west. He got a side view of the object which he described as cigar-shaped but bulkier, with a box-like structure underneath in the center.

Early the morning of August 1, a resident of Grosvenor Street in Dunedin reported seeing an airship. At one stage, he saw a bright yellow light shoot up what looked like a mast and stay at the top.

1908 - Sofia, Bulgaria: A very bright spherical object flew slowly above a square one afternoon.

1908 - Denmark: Many reported sightings of an 'airship' – 'an object with lights and wings' – were made in the skies over Denmark. Some commentators claimed that the object had been launched by British warships which were known to have been on exercise at the time in the North Sea.

1908 - Tunguska, Siberia: A mysterious fireball exploded over Tunguska in Siberia, creating shock waves felt miles away and that knocked down eighty-million trees. No impact crater or meteorite fragments have ever been found, but 1927, Russian scientists measured unusually high levels of radioactivity in the Tunguska soil. Speculation centers on the theory that a crippled alien spacecraft's nuclear reactor exploded on impact. This incident is thought to be the first modern crash by alien spacecraft.

1908 - Coast of Delaware: The English ship "Mohican," piloted by Capt. Urghart, was going to Philadelphia when it was surrounded by a thick, luminous cloud which “magnetized” everything on board. The compass was observed to swing wildly. When seamen tried to move some chains on the bridge, they found that they were glued to the metal floor. Suddenly the cloud rose and was seen above the sea for some time.

1908 - Bridgewater, Massachusetts: A spherical black UFO with a brilliant spotlight hovers and flies over. Seen by John E, Flynn, Philip S. Prophett and others.

1908 - Tacoma, Washington: On two consecutive evenings, a reddish cigar-shaped object ‘two or three times as bright as Jupiter’ flew over Kent, Washington; the same week, other residents described ‘colored lights’ and ‘a rocket at high altitudes’. Some newspapers proposed that a Japanese spy device was involved.

1907 - Burlington, Vermont: A torpedo-shaped UFO explodes over downtown Burlington, Vermont. Seen by Bishop John S. Michaud, former governor Alexander Woodbury, A.A. Buell and others.

1906 - Newfoundland, Canada: In the North Atlantic, NE of Newfoundland, deck of the ship St Andrew. “I saw three meteors fall into the water dead ahead of the ship one after another at a distance of about five miles. Although it was daylight, they left a red streak in the air from zenith to the horizon. Simultaneously the third engineer shouted to me. I then saw a huge meteor on the port beam falling in a zigzag manner less than a mile away to the southward. We could distinctly hear the hissing of water as it touched. It fell with a rocking motion leaving a broad red streak in its wake. The meteor must have weighed several tons, and appeared to be 10 to 15 feet in diameter. It was saucer shaped which probably accounted for the peculiar rocking motion. When the mass of metal struck the water the spray and steam rose to a height of at least 40 feet, and for a few moments looked like the mouth of a crater. If it had been night, the meteor would have illuminated the sea for 50 or 60 miles."

1906 - China Sea: Giant luminous wheels were seen by a British steamer.

1906 - Syracuse, New York: "Mystery meteor" performs weird aerial maneuvers.

1905 - Cherbourg, France: Sighting of an oval, reddish colored object that hung in the sky over this northern French port for several days. It was not in the position of the planet Venus, and was not reported from other towns.

1905 - Bucovina, Romania: During the evening a retired doctor saw a brightly glowing elongated, saucer-shaped object bigger than the moon traveling steadily westwards.

1905 - Silshee, California: At 1:30 am, J.A. Jackson noticed a bright light heading toward him in the sky. The light was also seen by the postmaster at the nearby town of Imperial. As the light neared him, Jackson made out the form of an 'airship' (although it had no gas balloon), showing several lights and apparently propelled by flapping wings.

1905 - Portland, Oregon: A buzzing UFO descends from heavy overcast and flies over Oregon.

1905 - Llangollen, Wales: Several witnesses saw a dark object in the sky that, observed through binoculars, had short wings and legs, and moved 'casually inclining sideways.' It reminded some witnesses of 'a huge winged pig, with webbed feet.'

1904 - Korea: "Three objects appeared beneath the clouds, their color a rather bright red. As they approached the ship they appeared to soar, passing above the broken clouds. After rising above the clouds they appeared to be moving directly away from the earth. The largest had an apparent area of about six suns. It was egg-shaped, the larger end forward. The second was about twice the size of the sun, and the third, about the size of the sun. Their near approach to the surface appeared to be most remarkable. That they did come below the clouds and soar instead of continuing their southeasterly course is also curious. The lights were in sight for over two minutes and were carefully observed by three people whose accounts agree as to the details." Sighting by the U.S.S. Supply off of the eastern coast of Korea, as reported by then Lt. Frank H. Schofield, later to become Commander-in-Chief of the Pacific Fleet.

1904 - Rolling Prairie, Indiana: Tom Darby, with his brother and mother, saw two whitish-blue objects about 400 m away, from a point situated 3 km north of Rolling Prairie. The objects hovered 2 or 3 m above ground, flew toward a barn, came closer to each other, and were hidden from view by a hill.

1903 - Argenteuil, France: At 11:00 pm, M. Desmoulins and four others saw a red object travel over 4 miles in 20 minutes. Seen through field glasses, the object did not appear to be a balloon.

1903 - Iola, Kansas: A large alien seven feet tall with long hair, horns and huge bulging eyes appears and is chased away by coal miners.

1902 - Devon, England: A Colonel Marwick reported a sighting of numerous 'highly colored objects like little suns or toy balloons.

1902 - Gulf of Guinea: Three persons aboard the "Fort Salisbury," including Second Officer A. H. Raymer, saw a huge, dark object bearing lights in the sea ahead. It was observed sinking slowly. Estimated length: 200 m.

1902 - Boschof, Oranjevrystaat, South Africa: Unusual sky booms heard over Boschof, Oranjevrystaat, South Africa.

***

The early twentieth century had its share of UFO encounters, the majority of which were mainly in keeping with the similar shapes of later periods; disk or saucer shaped objects, cigar shaped objects and round or spherical objects. However, a few uncommon shapes were reported, including ovals, rectangles, triangles, cruciforms and objects with apparent wings. A number of the craft appeared to be amphibious, either rising from or disappearing into bodies of water. One object was shot down by the German Luftwaffe. It was not reported whether materials or occupants were recovered from this crash.

The Great Airship Flap of 1897

Before continuing our chronology back into the 19th century, we will examine the year 1897, for reasons that will become clear momentarily, and skip for now the years 1898 and 1899, which we will return to shortly.

In 1896-1897 a plethora of highly consistent UFO sightings were reported on by the press across the American Midwest, beginning in California, then moving across the country.

1896, November 25 - Sacramento, California: A mysterious light was seen moving rapidly from the Northeast and heading in a southwesterly direction. As it neared the southern boundary of the city of Sacramento it turned directly toward the west and after passing the city went south, being distinctly visible for upward of 20 minutes.

Later that same day, in San Francisco, California, Hundreds of witnesses saw a large, cigar-shaped object, shining brilliant beams of light, and moving northwest passing over Oakland. The object was observed by many prominent individuals including Deputy Secretary of State George A. McCalvy, District Attorney Frank D. Ryan, and E. D. McCabe, the governor's personal secretary.

The following day, November 26, an airship that looked like a great black cigar with a fishlike tail neared Lorin District (Berkeley), California at tremendous speed. It turned quickly and disappeared in the direction of San Francisco. The body was at least 100 feet long and attached to it was a triangular tail, one apex being attached to the main body. The surface of the airship looked as if it were made of aluminum, which exposure to wind and weather had turned dark. Later that day, the witnesses saw it return.

There is now a period of perhaps a few weeks without any sightings until sometime later in Canada. First, two fishermen in coastal BC saw a pear-shaped flying craft. The next sighting is in Winnipeg, Canada: Approaching from the west, a mysterious airship flew over Winnipeg in full view of many citizens for a full fifteen minutes. After following the Assiniboine River and passing over St. Boniface Hospital, the UFO veered sharply to the north and was lost from view as it flew toward the town of Stony Mountain.

Again, there is a gap in sightings until a sudden rash spanning South Dakota, Nebraska, Kansas, Iowa, Missouri, Illinois, Indiana, Arkansas, and finally ending in Texas where the craft reportedly crashed and was destroyed.

South Dakota

Howard-Artesian, South Dakota: A flying object followed a train, coming closer and closer to the ground, as reported by the engineer, Joe Wright.

Nebraska

Hastings, Nebraska: A flying object was seen the morning of Sunday, January 24, 1897. It circled for a few minutes and then zoomed away to the north.

Omaha, Nebraska: On March 28, the majority of the population observed an object arriving from the southeast. It looked like a huge light, flew northwestward slowly, coming to a low altitude.

Kansas

Everest, Kansas: On April 1, the whole town saw an object fly under the cloud ceiling. It came down slowly, then flew away very fast to the southeast. When directly over the town it swept the ground with a powerful light. It was seen to rise at fantastic speed until barely discernible, then to come down again and sweep low over the witnesses. At one point it remained stationary for 5 minutes at the edge of a low cloud, which it illuminated. All could clearly see the silhouette of the craft.

LeRoy, Kansas: From a sworn statement dated Wednesday, April 21, a prosperous and prominent farmer named Alexander Hamilton told of an attack upon his cattle at about 10:30 PM the previous Monday, April 19. He, his son, and his tenant grabbed axes and ran some 700 feet from the house to the cow lot where a great cigar-shaped ship about 300 feet long floated some 30 feet above his cattle. It had a carriage underneath which was brightly lighted within, and which had numerous windows. Inside were six strange looking beings speaking in a foreign language. These beings suddenly became aware of Hamilton and the others. They immediately turned a searchlight on the farmer, and turned on some power, which sped up a turbine wheel (about 30 ft diameter) located under the craft. The ship rose, taking with it a two-year old heifer, which was roped about the neck by a cable of one-half inch thick, red material. The next day a neighbor, Link Thomas, found the animal's hide, legs and head in his field. He was mystified at how the remains got to where they were because of the lack of tracks in the soft soil. Alexander Hamilton's sworn statement was accompanied by an affidavit as to his veracity. The affidavit was signed by ten of the local leading citizens.

Iowa

Sioux City, Iowa: Robert Hibbard was caught by an anchor dropped from an unknown flying machine 22 km north of the town. He was dragged over 10 m and fell as his clothes were torn.

Linn Grove, Iowa: A large object was seen to fly slowly toward the north. It seemed ready to land and shortly thereafter, five witnesses found the craft on the ground, but then it spread its four giant wings and rose towards the North. Two strange figures aboard the craft made efforts to conceal themselves. Witnesses were surprised at the length of their hair. Most residents of Linn Grove saw the craft in flight.

Waterloo, Iowa: An airship, or a large vessel designed to leave the impression that it is a flying machine, was first observed here at dawn yesterday. The stranger in charge says it is a flying machine and he landed here to make some repairs and that he will resume his voyage in the air today. He keeps all people at a distance of several hundred yards from the machine and therefore many do not credit his story, but think it is a fake designed to create a sensation. The structure is about 40 feet long, constructed like a giant cigar, with wing-like attachments on the sides and a steering apparatus in the rear. The whole is surmounted by a cupola, or lookout cabin, on the roof. The queer craft appears to be built of canvas and to be heavily varnished."

Missouri

Kansas City, Missouri: 10,000 residents saw a large black ship hover overhead, flash green-blue and white lights, then moved straight up into space rapidly. Many other UFO sightings were reported, describing cigar-shaped, metallic craft with either wings, propellers, fins, or search lights. Bright lights were seen during the night.

Illinois

Hersman, Illinois: A passenger train on the Wabash line, bound for Quincy, was followed by a low-flying object for 15 min between Perry Springs and Hersman. All the passengers saw the craft, which had a red and white light. After Hersman it flew ahead of the train and disappeared rapidly.

Downs Township, Illinois: While working in his field, Haney Savidge saw an aerial craft land near him. Six people emerged from it and spoke to him for a few minutes before leaving again.

Girard, Illinois: On April 12, a large crowd of miners saw an unknown object land. The night operator of the Chicago-and-Alton Railroad, Paul McCramer, stated that he came sufficiently close to the craft to see a man emerge from it to repair the machinery. Traces were found over a large area. The object itself was elongated like a ship with a roof and a double canopy. It left toward the north.

Nilwood, Illinois: On the property of Z. Thacker, an unknown object landed on Apr. 12. Before the three witnesses could reach it, the craft, which was shaped like a cigar with a dome, rose slowly and left majestically toward the north. Witnesses: Edward Teeples, William Street and Franklin Metcalf.

Indiana

Gas City, Indiana: An object landed south of Gas City on the property of John Roush, terrifying the farmers and causing the horses and cattle to stampede. Six occupants of the ship came out and seemed to make some repairs. Before the crowd could approach the object, it rose rapidly and flew toward the east.

Michigan

Williamston, Michigan: At least a dozen farmers saw an object maneuver in the sky for an hour before it landed. A strange man near 3 m tall, almost naked and suffering from the heat, was the pilot of the craft. "His talk, while musical, seemed to be a repetition of bellowing." One farmer went near him and received a blow that broke his hip.

Ohio

Cleveland, Ohio: Joseph Singler, captain of the "Sea Wing," was fishing with S. H. Davis, of Detroit, when they saw on the lake what they thought was a ship, about 13 m long, with a canopy. A man, who they judged to be about 25 years old, wearing a hunting jacket and a cap, was fishing from the deck of the craft. Near him were a woman and a child who appeared to be around ten years old. When the "Sea Wing" came close to the craft, a large, colored balloon rose from the object, which lifted the craft up with it to an altitude of about 150 m. It then circled "like a hawk" before flying away.

Arkansas

Homan, Arkansas: Capt. James Hooton was hunting in the vicinity of Homan when he heard the noise of a steam engine and found an object in a clearing. It looked like a cylinder with pointed ends, lateral wheels, and horizontal blade over it. Hooton spoke with a man who wore dark glasses and walked behind the craft. There were three or four occupants. The witness was told this was indeed "The Airship" and that it used compressed air for propulsion. Hooton saw the wheels spin as the craft rose and flew away.

Hot Springs, Arkansas: Two police officers, Sumpter and McLenore, were riding northwest of Hot Springs when they saw a bright light in the sky. About 7 km farther they saw the light again coming down to the ground. One km farther the horses refused to walk. Two men were seen carrying lights. The lawmen took their rifles, called the strangers, and were told that they crossed the country with a flying craft. The silhouette of the machine, about 20 meters long, could be seen in the clearing. There was a woman with an umbrella nearby. It was raining, and the younger of the men was filling a large container with water. The elder man had a beard and suggested that the policemen fly with them "to a place where it does not rain." The same witnesses went back through the same spot 40 minutes later and found nothing.

McKinney Bayou, Arkansas: Judge Lawrence A. Byrne of Texarkana, Arkansas, was surveying a tract of land when he saw a peculiar object anchored on the ground. It was manned by three men who spoke a foreign language, and whom Byrne assumed might be Asian.

Texas

Hillsboro, Texas: A lawyer was surprised to see a lighted object fly over. His horse was scared and nearly toppled the carriage. When the main light was turned off, a number of smaller lights became visible on the underside of the dark object, which supported an elongated canopy. It went down toward a hill to the south. When the witness was on his way back one hour later he saw the object rising. It reached the altitude of the cloud ceiling and flew to the northeast at a fantastic speed with periodic flashes of light.

Josserand, Texas: Frank Nichols, a respected citizen, was awakened by a machine noise. Looking outside, he saw a heavy, lighted object land in his wheat field. He walked toward it and was stopped by two men who asked permission to draw water from his well. He then had a discussion with a half-dozen men, the crew of the strange machine. He was told how it worked but could not follow the explanation.

Merkel, Texas: People returning from church (presumably on Sunday morning, therefore we can deduce a date of April 11, 1897) observed a heavy object being dragged along the ground by a rope attached to a flying craft. The rope got caught in a railroad track. The craft was too high for its structure to be visible, but protrusions and a light could be distinguished. After about 10 min a man came down along the rope cut the end free, and went back aboard the craft, which flew away toward the northeast. The man was small and dressed in a light-blue uniform.

Rockland, Texas: John M. Barclay saw a flying object circling 5 m above ground. Elongated with protrusions and blinding lights, it went dark when it landed. Barclay was met by a man who told him his purpose was peaceful and requested some common hardware items to repair the craft.

Aurora, Texas: Early on April 17, the ship crashed into a windmill in Aurora. Apparently, the repeated repairs were insufficient, and the craft was no longer able to operate effectively. Some debris was scattered in the wreck and was salvaged by onlookers, and a single body was buried in the local cemetery, complete with a funeral ceremony. Documents were recovered but no one was able to decipher their contents.

A Windmill Demolishes It.

Aurora, Wise Co., Tex., April 17.—(To The News.)—About 6 o'clock this morning the early risers of Aurora were astonished at the sudden appearance of the airship which has been sailing through the country.

It was traveling due north, and much nearer the earth than ever before. Evidently some of the machinery was out of order, for it was making a speed of only ten or twelve miles an hour and gradually settling toward the earth. It sailed directly over the public square, and when it reached the north part of town collided with the tower of Judge Proctor's windmill and went to pieces with a terrific explosion, scattering debris over several acres of ground, wrecking the windmill and water tank and destroying the judge's flower garden.

The pilot of the ship is supposed to have been the only one on board, and while his remains are badly disfigured, enough of the original has been picked up to show that he was not an inhabitant of this world.

Mr. T. J. Weems, the United States signal service officer at this place and an authority on astronomy, gives it as his opinion that he was a native of the planet Mars.

Papers found on his person—evidently the record of his travels—are written in some unknown hieroglyphics, and can not be deciphered.

The ship was too badly wrecked to form any conclusion as to its construction or motive power. It was built of an unknown metal, resembling somewhat a mixture of aluminum and silver, and it must have weighed several tons.

The town is full of people to-day who are viewing the wreck and gathering specimens of the strange metal from the debris. The pilot's funeral will take place at noon to-morrow. S. E. HAYDON.

We have reproduced the likely path of the craft across the country by analyzing the data including dates of sightings and direction of travel mentioned by observers. It should be noted that in many cases the craft seems to have been slowly making its way over the landscape in a zig-zag fashion, as if performing some type of inspection or survey of the land. The broad sweeps of its journey are depicted in the following map. The dates and distances between each sighting are consistent with the apparent capabilities of the ship.

The biggest discrepancy in my mind is that of the ship's inhabitants. Many sightings agree that there were up to six occupants. Most of the earlier sightings site these beings as speaking an unknow language, however, as the ship began to require repairs, the occupants began speaking to the locals in English to facilitate the gathering of supplies. Only one fact remains unexplained. Why was there only one body recovered from the crash? This might be an indication that the other bodies were burned up.

Another possible explanation is that the other crew members had already disembarked from the craft, possibly to blend into the local population, or to pose as ordinary travelers.

In 1973, the International UFO Bureau interviewed a ninety-one-year-old local woman in Aurora, who had been a girl of fifteen at the time of the reported incident. She said her parents had gone to the site of the crash but had refused to take her along. She apparently had been allowed to attend the funeral however, for she recalled that the remains of the pilot, "a small man," had been buried in the Aurora cemetery. The International UFO Bureau then initiated legal proceedings to exhume the body of the pilot, however, their efforts were thwarted by the Aurora Cemetery Association.

19th Century

1899, November 1 - Dordogne, Dourite, France: An object 'like an enormous star' was seen from 7:00 pm, 'at times white, then red, and sometimes blue… moving like a kite' in the southerly sky.

1899 - Luzarches, France: M.A. Garry observed a round luminous object rise above the horizon and shrink in size as it moved into the distance over 15 minutes.

1899 - South Africa: The Transvaal government was inundated with sighting reports of phantom airships, often equipped with powerful searchlights.

Note. This was four years before the Wright brothers invented the airplane.

1899 - Prescott, Arizona: Dr. Warren E. Day observed a luminous object that 'traveled with the Moon all day' until 2:00 pm. A similar object had been observed the day before from Tonto, Arizona.

1899 - El Paso, Texas: A luminous object was seen in daylight from 10:00am to 4:00pm; Venus was two months past its secondary phase of maximum brilliance.

1898 - Lille, France: An astronomer saw through his telescope a rectangular object with a violet-colored band on one side, the rest being striped red and black. It was not in the position of any known planet. It remained stationary for 10 minutes, then 'cast out sparks and disappeared.'

1896 - Arolla, Switzerland: Author Aleister Crowley was walking in the mountains when he suddenly saw two little men. He made a gesture to them, but they did not seem to pay attention and disappeared among the rocks.

1895 - Oxford, England: A disk was seen rising above some trees and disappearing into the east

1893 - North China Sea: The ship, H.M.S. Carolina was sailing in the North China Sea, when a report from an officer of unusual light activity in the sky came to the attention of Captain J.N. Norcross. The officer told Captain Norcross that the lights appeared sometimes in a huge mass, other times spread out in unusual patterns. He said that they resembled Chinese lanterns set between the masts of a ship. The next night these strange lights reappeared but with a reddish glow and emanating small amounts of smoke.

1892 - Netherlands: An astronomer called Muller was observing the moon through his telescope when a black disk moved across his field of view.

1892 - Poland: Phantom airships were encountered appearing at night and usually equipped with powerful searchlights.

1891 - Crawfordsville, Indiana: As reported in the Brooklyn Eagle newspaper on September 10, 1891, two icemen were working outside in Crawfordsville at about 2:00am five nights previously, when a bizarre object sailed overhead. The icemen described the UFO as a 'seemingly headless monster', although there is no reason to believe that it was an animal of any kind. It was about 20 ft long, and 8ft wide, moving in the sky toward the two men, and 'seemingly propelled by fin-like attachments.' The men moved, and the UFO flew off. The noise awoke Methodist pastor G.W. Swittze, who saw it circling in the sky.

1888 - Ragusa, Italy: From the 'Memoirs' of the Minor Brothers, "Luminous bodies were seen flying through the sky in lines for one hour."

1887 - Cape Race, Nova Scotia: On November 12, 1887, at midnight, near, a huge ball of fire appeared, slowly emerging from the ocean to an altitude of sixteen to seventeen meters. This sphere started moving against the wind and stopped close to the ship from which it was observed. Then it rushed away in the sky and disappeared in the southeast. The whole observation had lasted five minutes.

1886 - Venezuela: During the night of the 24th of October last, which was rainy and tempestuous, a family of nine persons, sleeping in a hut a few leagues from Maracaibo, were awakened by a loud humming noise and a vivid, dazzling light, which brilliantly illuminated the interior of the house. The occupants completely terror stricken, and believing, as they relate, that the end of the world had come, threw themselves on their knees and commenced to pray, but their devotions were almost immediately interrupted by violent vomiting, and extensive swellings commenced to appear in the upper part of their bodies, this being particularly noticeable about the face and lips. It is to be noted that the brilliant lights were not accompanied by a sensation of heat, although there was a smoky appearance and a peculiar smell. The next morning, the swellings had subsided, leaving upon the face and body large black blotches. No trace of lightning could afterward by observed in any part of the building, and all the sufferers unite in saying that there was no detonation, but only the loud humming already mentioned. Another curious attendant circumstance is that the trees around the house showed no signs of injury until the ninth day, when they suddenly withered. From Warner Cowgill, U. S. Consulate, Maracaibo, Venezuela in a letter posted in Scientific American, Dec 18.

1885 - Constantinople, Turkey: On November 1, at 9:30pm, there was seen, west of Adrianople, an elongated object giving off a strong luminosity. It seemed to float in the air and its apparent disk was four or five times larger than the full moon. It traveled slowly and cast light on the whole camp behind the station with a brightness about ten times greater than a large electric bulb. In the morning, at dawn, a very luminous flame, first bluish, then greenish, and moving at a height of five to six meters, made a series of turns around the ferryboat pier at Scutari. Its blinding luminosity lighted the street and flooded the inside of the houses with light.

1884 - Dundy County, Nebraska: Four cowboys heard a whirring noise overhead then saw a cylindrical object crash into the ground.

1883 - Segeberg, Germany: A teacher and children at a school all saw two fiery balls in a clear sky one day. The size of two full moons, the objects traveled slowly together from north to south.

1883 - Zacatecas, Mexico: An astronomer at the Zacatecas Observatory saw 143 circular objects cross in front of the sun. The astronomer, Professor Jose' Bonilla, managed to take a photograph of one of the objects. He wrote up his finding, which were sent to the French journal L'Astronomie.

1882 - England: A huge disc was observed by numerous people in England during the night, traveling across the sky in an east-west direction. A number of eminent scientists witnessed the object, among them being Dr E Walter Maunder, Greenwich astronomer; English spectroscopist, J Rand Capron; Dutch astronomers Audemans and Zeeman. The Royal Observatory, Greenwich published a report of the conclusions reached by scientists, following the appearance of what had been termed, "The Great Saucer". The report had this to say: "It appeared to be well defined in body and the inference drawn was that it was a meteor, not in the old vague sense of some object high in the Earth's atmosphere, but in the sense of a solid cosmological substance, disc-like in appearance, the orbit of which brought it within the terrestrial atmosphere. But nothing could be more unlike the rush of a great meteor or fireball, with intense radiance and fiery train. The advance of this object, though swift, appeared to be orderly and controlled. There was no sign of the compression of the atmosphere before it, no hint that the matter composing its front part, was in anyway more strongly heated than the rest of its substance, if substance, indeed it possessed."

1881 - Australia: Between Melbourne and Sydney at sea. The two sons of the Prince of Wales, (one of them the future king of England, King George V), were cruising aboard "*La Bacchante*" when an object resembling a fully lighted ship was seen, which they described as "a phantom vessel all aglow."

1881 - Americus, Georgia: Mr. Z. T. Baisden, of Americus, gives us the following story of a whirlwind that visited his place, scaring all his hands and some visitors very badly. A whirlwind occurred in a twelve acre cornfield that was about four feet in diameter and sometimes a hundred feet high. The body of it was perfectly black, with fire in the center and emitted a strong sulphureous vapor that could be smelt three hundred yards from it. The whirlwind would divide into three and move rapidly over the field, twisting up the corn stalks by the roots and carrying them up. These three minor whirlwinds would then come together with a loud crash, cracking and burning and shoot high up into the heavens. Three young ladies who were visiting Mrs. Baisden went in about 150 feet to observe it, but received such a shower of burning sand upon their face and necks that they ran affrighted to the house. Mr. Baisden says that he cannot account for this strange phenomenon, and it certainly frightened all who saw it. The strange part was that it contained fire, yet did not appear to burn the corn that it did not tear up, and its sulphurous vapor sickened and burnt all who got close enough to get a full breath of it.

1880 - Aldershot, England: A strange being dressed in tight-fitting clothes and shining helmet soared over the heads of two sentries, who fired without result. The flying entity then stunned the guards with something described as blue fire.

1880 - France: A member of the French Academy observed a glittering, white gold cigar-shaped object in the sky that had pointed ends.

1880 - the Persian Gulf: The British steamer Patna was traversing the waters of the gulf when around midnight, two enormous glowing wheels each estimated to be 500 to 600 meters in diameter appeared underwater on each side of the ship. The wheels were spinning, one on each side with the spokes touching the ship. The sighting lasted 20 minutes and was witnessed by Captain Avern, third officer Manning, and Lee Fort Brace.

1880 - St. Petersburg, Russia: A large, illuminated globe, accompanied by two smaller lights is seen to follow a ravine outside the city.

1880 - Lamy, New Mexico: Four men walking near Galisteo Junction were surprised as they heard voices coming from a "strange balloon," which flew over them. It was shaped like a fish and seemed to be guided by a large fanlike device. There were eight to ten figures aboard. Their language was not understood. The object flew low over Galisteo Junction and rose rapidly toward the east.

1880 Venezuela: A 14-year-old boy saw a luminous ball descending from the sky and hovering near him. He felt somehow "drawn" to it but succeeded in backing away in spite of his terror.

***

From 1880 to 1900, all across the United States and Europe, thousands of witnesses sighted flying machines resembling dirigibles, which were not produced by factories until twenty years later. In most cases, it was a matter of voluminous, fusiform, vessels equipped with powerful searchlights, often emitting engine sounds, and, in some cases, even seeming to have propellers. In the United States, the majority of the sightings occurred between 1896 and 1897. Other cases were reported, particularly in Spain, Germany, Sweden, and Russia. A second wave of sightings occurred at the turn of the century in Great Britain.

The fact remains that the first efficient aircraft were subsequent to 1910, and even the Zeppelins built during World War I lacked the capabilities observed by the witnesses to these phenomena.

***

1879 - Persian Gulf: The S.S. Vulture crew reported, two luminous rotating wheels, about 130 ft. across, seen above the water before diving

1878 - Texas: John Martin, a farmer, spotted a fast moving dark object high in the southern sky. When it passed overhead, he saw that it was the size of a 'large saucer'. It continued on its way and was soon lost to view. In recounting the event, a local newspaper remarked, 'Mr. Martin is a gentleman of undoubted veracity and this strange occurrence, if it was not a balloon, deserves the attention of our scientists'.

1877 - Venice: Fiery spheres, extremely luminous, came out of a cloud of peculiar shape and went slowly toward the north for one hour.

1875 - Prague, Czechoslovakia: A Professor Schafarick saw "an object of such strange nature that I do not know what to say about it. It was of a blinding white and crossed slowly the face of the moon. It remained visible afterwards."

1874 - Oaxaca, Mexico: Residents saw a huge, gently swaying, trumpet-shaped object estimated to be 425 feet long hovering in the sky for six minutes.

1873 - Bonham, Texas: A huge cigar-shaped object swooped low over the town in broad daylight, then disappeared quickly to the east.

1872 - Banbury, England: At King's Sutton an object resembling a haystack flew on an irregular course. Sometimes high, sometimes very low, it was accompanied by fire and dense smoke. It produced the same effect as a tornado, felling trees and walls. It suddenly vanished.

1871 - Meudon Observatory, France: Astronomer Trouvelot noted a number of spherical objects in the sky. Among the objects he saw was a circle that first seemed about to fall, then descended "like a disk falling through water."

1870 - African Coast: Capt. F.W. Banner and crew reported "A semi-circle divided into four parts, and a central shaft extending far outward & curving backward emitted vivid shafts of light."

1870 - Atlantic Ocean: An object was seen from the ship *Lady of the Lake* that appeared to be a light-gray colored disk that flew against the wind.

1869 - Ashland, Tennessee: A whirlwind came along over the neighboring woods, taking up small branches and leaves of trees and burning them in a sort of flaming cylinder that traveled at a rate of about five miles an hour, increasing in size as it traveled. It passed directly over the spot where a team of horses were feeding and singed their manes and tails up to the roots. It then swept towards the house, taking a stack of hay in its course. It seemed to increase in heat as it went, and by the time it reached the house it immediately fired the shingles from end to end of the building, so that in ten minutes the whole dwelling was wrapped in flames. The tall column of traveling caloric then continued its course over a wheat field that had been recently cradled, setting fire to all the stacks that happened to be in its course. Passing from the field, its path lay over a stretch of woods, which reached the river. The green leaves on the trees were crisped to a cinder for a breadth of

20 yards, in a straight line to the Cumberland. When the "pillar of fire" reached the water, it suddenly changed its route down the river, raising a column of steam which went up to the clouds for about half-a-mile, when it finally died out. Not less than 200 people witnessed this strangest of strange phenomena, and all of them tell substantially the same story about it. Symon's Monthly Meteorological Magazine, 1869

1868 - Copiago, Chile: A strange "aerial construction bearing lights and making engine noises flew low over this town. Local people also described it as a giant bird covered with large scales producing a metallic noise.

1868 - Oxford, England: Astronomers at Radcliffe Observatory saw a luminous object that moved quickly across the sky, stopped, changed course to the west, then to the south, where it hovered for four minutes, then headed toward the north.

1862 - Indian Ocean: A shipwrecked Danish sailor reported seeing a strange aircraft as large as a battleship with four huge wings. This object was seen to crash into a cliff and was destroyed.

April 19, 1861 – Annapolis, Maryland: the 7th New York Militia were travelling by steamboat when they saw a UFO following their vessel. They described it as round and surrounded by three glowing circles.

1860 - Shreveport, Louisiana: "Our attention was called to a strange light in the heavens. Ongoing out into the gallery we had a magnificent view of it. It appeared to the naked eye, about 300 yards in length, extending from North to West appearing just above the tallest trees. Its color was that of a red-hot stove. From the center, beautiful rays resembling those of the sun drawing water would ascend to a considerable height, the whole presenting a very beautiful and sublime appearance. We watched it for about an hour without perceiving it to change any.

1847 - London, England: A spherical craft was spotted rising vertically through the clouds.

1846 - USA: A 'luminous flying disc' was reported over this eastern seaboard area.

1845 - Naples, Italy: Astronomers at a Naples observatory recorded the appearance of several luminous discs, which left trails.

1843 - Warwick, England: A remarkable cloud passed over Warwick and Charles Cooper reported seeing three beings in the sky.

1842 - Orenburg, Soviet Union: Small metal objects, perfectly hexagonal, fell out of the sky after a "strange cloud" appeared.

1836 - Cherbourg, France: A 'gleaming aerial vessel' was seen in the sky overhead.

1833 - Niagara Falls, Canada: A large, square, luminous object was seen for more than an hour over Niagara Falls.

1831 - Thuringia, Germany: It was reported that a brilliant luminous disc was seen in the night sky.

1826 - English Channel. Sailors in the Channel reported seeing a gray, torpedo-shaped object flying overhead.

1825 - Poland, Ohio: A brilliant object was visible in the sky for more than an hour.

1820 - Embrun, France; A formation of flying objects crossed the French town. Francois Arago wrote of this date in the 'Annales de chimie et de physique': "Numerous observers have seen, during an eclipse of the moon, strange objects moving in straight lines. They were equally spaced and remained in line when they made turns. Their movements made a military precision."

1819 - Amhurst, Massachusetts: A white silvery fireball light accompanied by a violent explosion was seen. Afterwards, a gelatinous substance was said to have been found.

1816 - Edinburgh, Scotland: Many people saw a large, luminous crescent-shaped object flying over the city.

1812 - Bucovina, Romania: The war between the Russians, French and Germans, over the town of Bucovina. "Towards noon a large star with many rays appeared and in the night she ascended higher and flew in the direction of the Russians; afterwards she returned and went to the west, where the beams were extinguished. Thus did the star reveal herself for four months."

1808 - Piedmont, France: Formation of 'luminous discs' observed in the sky.

1803 - Barsdorf, Germany: What was recorded, as a shooting star got larger and larger until it fell to earth between Barsdorf and Freiburg. A whizzing noise was heard as it passed close to the ground before it landed and then lay burning. Next day a jelly-like mass was found on the snow.

1800 - Baton Rouge, Louisiana: A bright red object the size of a house flew over the city and was seen by many spectators. It created a violent rushing noise as it shot off over the forest and crashed amidst the woods, creating a large crater, and the sensation of an earthquake. This event was reported on by then-vice-president Thomas Jefferson, who named as his source one William Dunbar of Baton Rouge, Louisiana.

***

The 19th Century exhibited all the usual shapes and colors of UFO, mainly discs or spheres, but also included several sightings of "pillars or fire" or "whirlwinds" which left a path of destruction in their wake. Oddly, some encounters left behind a gelatinous substance. Winged ships with strange men aboard were witnessed across North America.

18th Century

1799 - Hereford, England: A "large red pillar of fire" was seen in the sky going south. It was preceded by "flashes of extremely vivid electrical sort". Other objects were seen leaving luminous trails.

1799 - Huncoates and Lincolnshire, England: A ball of fire passed in the sky.

1799 - England: A "beautiful ball blazing with white light" was seen. It made no sound and red sparks flew from it.

1796 - Dresden and Berlin, Germany: A bright light irregular in form and the size of the moon was seen in the sky above. A large detonation was heard, and a dark bituminous substance fell to earth.

1793 - Northumberland, England: A bright oval light was observed in the sky overhead for around five minutes. At first it appeared the size of Sirius.

1790 - Alencon, France: Police Inspector Liabeuf witnessed and investigated a large red globe as it flew over farmland. The globe landed and a man came out and spoke in a language none understood. The globe then exploded, and the man disappeared. The event was witnessed by many and is well documented.

***

In 1789, American founding father John Adams financed a publication entitled "A Short Account of the

Solar System, and of Comets in General". The document outlined the national security implications of comets, detailing the probabilities and potential effects such as fires and floods, should the comet strike Earth. The book explained that these comets were quite possibly inhabited by intelligent beings, who might be a problem because they were almost certainly more knowledgeable about the universe than people on Earth.

***

1787 - Edinburgh, Scotland: A bright fireball light like the sun was seen traveling horizontally through the sky at. It dropped a little, then rose again, bursting behind a cloud.

1786 - England: A bright ball of fire and light lasting 40 minutes was seen in the sky over southern England during a hurricane of wind.

1783 - England: The scientist Tiberius Cavallo was a witness to a sighting that also stunned Royal guests at a celebration to mark the birth of the 15th child of King George III and Queen Charlotte. A luminous object appeared from beneath a cloud and soon became brilliantly lit before coming to a halt. According to Cavallo's account of the incident: "This strange sphere seemed at first to be pale blue in color, but its luminosity increased and soon it set off again towards the east." Even though the sun was shining the object is said to have lit up everything on the ground and eventually disappeared with a terrific explosion.

1783 - Greenwich, England: An object was observed that 'gave birth' to eight satellites, which disappeared slowly towards the Southeast.

1783 - Sudbrooke, England: Several people saw a luminous object hovering in the northeast at approximately 10 PM. It emitted fixed flashes of light, lightning, which lasted about 30 sec. The object then separated into seven or eight pieces and traveled swiftly horizontally before disappearing in an arc like a rocket.

1777 - France: French astronomer Charles Messier saw a number of dark round objects in the sky.

1768 - Germany: The German poet, dramatist, author and scientist Johann Goethe was himself a witness to a strange luminous object. He was journeying from Frankfurt to Leipzig by stagecoach. At one point the rough uphill track was so treacherous from mud and rain that the passengers were forced to alight and follow on behind. It was then that Goethe suddenly became aware of lights in the ravine below them. Writes Goethe: All of a sudden, in a ravine on the right-hand side of the track, I saw a sort of amphitheater, wonderfully illuminated. In a funnel-shaped space there were innumerable little lights shining, ranged step-fashion over one another; and they shone so brilliantly that the eye was dazzled. But the sight was even more confusing because these objects did not keep still, but jumped about here and there, as well as downwards from above." Goethe recounts elsewhere of the same trip, he and two other witnesses saw a type of large luminous tube positioned on the ground, surrounded by a multitude of small, very bright, moving flames.

1762 - Switzerland, Lausanne: A huge spindle-shaped object was seen crossing the sun by two different observatories and was observed by one astronomer nearly every day for a month.

1758 - Cambridge, England: A dazzling light as bright as day seemed to descend obliquely towards the earth, and then 'rose again with renewed splendor'.

1752 - Augermanland, Sweden: Luminous spheres were seen coming out of a bright cylinder.

1751 - Agram, Croatia: An iron meteorite crashed. The vapory cloud left by an aerial explosion was visible for an hour before it entirely dissipated. After the detonation took place, two masses of iron fell in the shape of chains welded together.

1749 - Japan: For four days three round objects were seen in the skies.

1742 - London, England: An account by a Fellow of the Royal Society: "I was crossing St James Park when a light rose from behind the trees and houses, from the south and west, which at first I thought was a rocket of large size. But when it rose 20 degrees, it moved parallel to the horizon, but waved like this (the speaker drew an undulating line) and went on in the direction of north-by-east. It seemed very near. Its motion was very slow. I had it for about half a mile in view. A light flame was turned backwards by the resistance the air made to it. From one of burning charcoal. That end was a frame like bars of iron, and quite opaque in my sight. At one point on the longitudinal frame, or cylinder, it issued a train in the shape of a tail of light more bright at one point on the rod or cylinder; so that it was transparent for more than half of its length. The head of this strange object seemed about a half a degree in diameter and the tail near three degrees in length."

1741 - London, England: Lord Beauchamp was in Kensington Gardens when he observed a ball of fire in the sky. It seemed as if it was eight inches in diameter but grew until it was about a yard and a half.

1733 - Dorset, England: Dec 8 – James Cracker of, a small town in Dorset, saw a silvery disc fly overhead in broad daylight. Here is his eyewitness account: "Something in the sky which appeared in the north but vanished from my sight, as it was intercepted by trees, from my vision. I was standing in a valley. The weather was warm, the sun shone brightly. Suddenly it re-appeared, darting in and out of my sight with an amazing coruscation. The color of this phenomenon was like burnished, or new-washed silver. It shot with speed like a star falling in the night. But it had a body much larger and a train longer than any shooting star I have seen. Next day Mr. Edgecombe informed me that he and another gentleman had seen this strange phenomenon at the same time as I had. It was about 15 miles from where I saw it, and steering a course from east to north."

1731 - Firrenze, Italy: Immediately before an earthquake a luminous cloud was seen in the sky. It was watched until it disappeared over the horizon.

1731 - Sheffield, England: Thomas Short saw what he later described as "a dark red cloud, below which was a luminous body which emitted intense beams of light. The light beams moved slowly for a while, then stopped. Suddenly it became so hot that I could take off my shirt even though I was outdoors" [in the dead of winter].

1731 - Kilkenny, Ireland: A great ball of fire was observed. It was reported that it shook that entire island and that the whole sky seemed to burst into flames.

1731 - Romania: There appeared in the west a great sign in the sky, blood red and very large. It stayed in place for two hours, separated into two parts which then rejoined, and the object disappeared toward the west.

1718 - India: A large fiery mass fell and exploded on the ground. Subsequently a jelly-like mass, silvery and scaly, was said to have been found.

1715 - England: Edmond Halley, the famed astronomer and physicist recalled two accounts involving unidentified crafts. Halley's second experience was 39 years after his first in 1676. Halley saw an object that hovered for more than two hours, seemingly in defiance of Newton's laws of motion and gravity.

***

Notable 18th century UFO experiences included several objects which were able to split and rejoin, several sightings which appeared coincident with earthquakes. One object reappeared daily for a month. Notable witnesses included Sir Edmond Halley, and the entire British court of King George III.

1694 - Montgomeryshire, Wales: "A fiery exhalation…a furlong broad" rose out of the sea burning straw, hay, and barns. Grass tainted, killing cattle, and skin affected.

1686 - Leipzig, Germany: A fiery ball of light was seen to travel east to west before hovering some seven minutes in the sky at an estimated altitude of 30 miles. It was about half the size of the moon and gradually vanished from view.

1680 - France: The government issued a commemorative coin of a UFO sighting.

1676 - England: Edmond Halley's first experience was in March of 1676, when he saw a "vast body apparently bigger than the moon." He estimated it at 40 mi. above him. He also stated that it made a noise, "Like the rattling of a great cart over stones." After estimating the distance, it traveled in a matter of minutes, he came to the conclusion that it moved at a speed greater than 9,600 m.p.h.

1663 - Robozero, Russia: A fiery ball of light stopped over a lake at, the noisy object gave out blue smoke and two beams of light projected ahead of it. Fishermen on the lake were burned by the intense heat. The object disappeared and returned about one hour later. It was observed by many groups of witnesses.

1649 - Hamburg, Germany: A fireball which "moved in bounds up and down" was observed.

1643 - England: From diarist, John Evelyn. “I must not forget what amazed us exceedingly the night before, namely, a shining cloud in the air in a shape resembling a sword, the point reaching to the north. It was as bright as the moon, the rest of the sky being very serene. It began about 11 at night and vanished not till about one, being seen by all the south of England.”

1619 - Fluelan, Switzerland: A prefect of a Swiss Canton saw a long, bright object flying along a lake near Fluelen.

1606 - Kyoto, Japan: A whirling ball of fire was seen hovering over Nijo Castle.

1593 - London, England: A “flying dragon” surrounded by flames was seen over the city.

1577 - Tubingen, Germany: “Objects came out of the clouds resembling large, tall and wide hats and they landed in great numbers and in a variety of colors.”

1569 - China: In the evening, a flaming star appeared in the sky. It was regarded as an omen of serious changes announcing the fall of the Chu Dynasty

1566 - Basel, Switzerland: Many black spheres were seen moving through the sky at great speed at around sunrise. August 7th is close to the peak of perhaps the largest meteor shower of the year, the Perseids, which can be very spectacular. It is tempting to try to link the Basel phenomena with the meteors, but it is unlikely that even the Perseids would produce enough rocks large enough to be seen as dark objects. Furthermore, large meteorites are generally observed as balls of fire, rather than dark objects, due to the heat generated upon entering the atmosphere.

1561 - Nuremberg, Germany: A large number of brightly colored spheres, disks, and cylinders seemed to wage a sort of battle in the sky. The event was seen by many people, leaving a profound psychological mark on the population and causing the authority's great concern.

1554 - France: "There appeared, about the moon, a burning fire, emitting a great noise, what seemed to be the point of a lance, turning from side to side, from east to west, casting out flames on all sides."

1529 - Prussia: Two burning suns were seen at Erfurt, Prussia. Then a great 'burning beam' landed suddenly. It took off again into the sky, where it became circular in shape.

1528 - Utrecht, Holland. "A cruel and strange sight was seen in the sky, which terrified the townspeople and made the enemy think he would get the city. It was the form of a Burgundian cross right over the city, high in the sky, yellow in color, and fearful to behold."

1517 - Moldavia, Romania: A large blue glowing disk appeared and remained in the sky for some time.

***

During the Renaissance, many fireballs were witnessed, most of which hovered over a particular area for some time. Other shapes were observed, including spheres, discs, cylinders and other extended shapes sometimes described as a sword or cross. On several occasions, people were injured by these flying objects, and on one occasion the objects seemed to be battling amongst themselves. In several of his paintings Leonardo DaVinci included flying vehicles as well as an alien or two. One has to wonder what a great mind as his was trying to relate to the history that was yet to come. His inventions were certainly ahead of his time by many centuries, perhaps he was trying to tell us of other aspects of our reality that were going to be revealed, or, perhaps he was just revealing what were already in the skies as well as walking among us already.

The Middle Ages

1492 - the Bahamas: Christopher Columbus and Pedro Gutierrez while on the deck of the Santa Maria, observed, "a light glimmering at a great distance." It vanished and reappeared several times during the night, moving up and down, "in sudden and passing gleams." It was sighted 4 hours before land was sighted and taken by Columbus as a sign they would soon come to land. (From *The Life and Voyages of Christopher Columbus* by Washington Irving)

1479 - Arabia: There is a woodcut of a UFO that was sighted over Arabia in an illustrated volume published in 1557. *The Prodigiorum Ac Ostentorum Chronicon*, text by Conrad Lycosthenes, is one of the best-illustrated books of the Renaissance depicting medieval superstition. On page 494 is a woodcut showing a spaceship seen over Arabia in 1479.

1468 - Japan: A dark object, which made a "sound like a wheel," flew from Mt. Kasuag toward the west at midnight.

1461 - Arras, France: A fiery thing like an iron rod of good length and as large as one half of the moon was seen in the sky for less than a quarter of an hour. This object was also described as being "shaped like a ship from which fire was seen flowing."

1458 - Japan: An object as bright as the full moon, followed by curious signs, was seen in the sky.

1453 - Constantinople: “A fire descended from the sky, stood over the city, and enveloped her with light all night long.” Written during the siege of Constantinople.

1394 - England: “A certain thing appeared in the likeness of fire in many parts of England every night. This fiery apparition, oftentimes when anybody went alone, it would go with him, and would stand still when he stood still. To some it appeared in the likeness of a turning wheel burning; to other some a round object, the likeness of a barrel, flashing out flames of fire at the head; to others, the likeness of a long burning lance.”

1387 - Northamptonshire, England: A fire in the sky, like a burning and revolving wheel, or round barrel of flame, emitting fire from above, and others in the shape of a long fiery beam, were seen through a great deal of the winter.

1361 - Japan: A flying object described as being “shaped like a drum, about twenty feet in diameter” emerged from the inland sea off the western Japanese coast.

1347 Europe: During the height of the Black Plague, (1347-1350) Reports from this period feature strange cigarlike objects flying low through the sky and dispersing noxious mists. Soon after these objects passed by, plague would break out in that area. Other features from this period similar to modern UFO reports include sightings of mysterious MIB-like scythe-wielding “reapers” clad in black hoods & robes, and mysteriously slaughtered cattle and other animals. One year before an outbreak of plague, a “column of fire” was seen over the Pope’s palace at

Avignon. A monstrous "whale" was cast ashore at Egemont shortly before another plague outbreak, and numerous times during this period "rumblings like thunder" were heard even when there were no storms. Blazing "comets" were seen numerous times in the heavens – some of which may have been real celestial objects frightening an omen-crazy populace – of which numerous were said to be accompanied by "flames" (aurorae?) hanging low in the sky.

1335 - Detchani, Yugoslavia: The monastery at Detchani, built between 1327 and 1335, is decorated with frescoes showing angels enclosed in sorts of vessels flying in the sky.

1332 - Uxbridge, England: There was seen in the sky a pillar of fire the size of a small boat, pallid and livid in color. It rose from the south, crossed the sky with a slow and grave motion, and went north. Out of the front of the pillar, a fervent red flame burst forth with great beams of light. Its speed increased, and it flew through the air.

1320 - Durham, England: After the abbot of Durham Abbey died and was buried, a strange light was seen to descend from the sky and move about over his grave.

1290 - Yorkshire, England: The Abbot and monks of Byland Abbey, (the largest Cistercian abbey in England), were about to commence a meal when one of the brethren ran in to announce a great portent outside. They all ran outside and saw a large silver disc fly slowly overhead, which caused utmost terror.

1271 - Japan: The famous priest Nichiren was about to be beheaded at Tatsunokuchi, Kamakura, when there appeared in the sky an object like a full moon, shiny and bright. The officials panicked and the execution was not carried out.

1270 - Bristol, England: A spaceship was seen, which landed and an occupant came down from a ladder and was suffocated in the Earth's atmosphere.

1254 - St Albans, England: Some monks saw in the night sky 'a kind of large ship elegantly shaped and well-equipped and of marvelous color'.

1239 - England: Matthew of Paris wrote: "On July 24 at dusk, but not when the stars came out, while the air was clear, serene and shining, a great star appeared. It was like a torch, rising from the south, and flying on both sides of it, there was emitted in the height of the sky a very great light. It turned quickly towards the north, not quickly, nor, indeed, with speed, but exactly as it wished to ascend to a place high in the air."

1235 - Japan: During the night while General Yoritsume and his army were encamped, mysterious lights were observed in the heavens. The lights were seen in the southwest for many hours, winging, circling and moving in loops. The general ordered a "full-scale scientific investigation" of these strange events. The report finally submitted to him has the "soothing" ring of many contemporary explanations offered for UFO phenomena. In essence it read: "the whole thing is completely natural, General. It is… only the wind making the stars sway."

1211 - Kent, England: During a Sunday mass it is said that the congregation saw an anchor descend and catch on a tombstone in the churchyard. The churchgoers rushed outside to see a strange 'ship' in the sky, with people on board. One occupant of the vessel leaped over the side but did not fall: 'as if swimming in water' he made his way through the air toward the anchor. The people on the ground tried to capture him. The man then 'hurried up to the ship.' His companions cut the anchor rope, and the ship then 'sailed out of sight.' The local blacksmith made ornaments from the abandoned anchor to decorate the church lectern.

1207 - Tilbury, England: Gervase of Tilbury writes in *Otio Imperialia* about an aerial ship which caught its anchor on a pile of stones. An occupant came down from the ship and managed to free it, however he was asphyxiated by the atmosphere.

1200 - England: William of Newburgh describes a silvery, flat, shiny disc-like object, which appeared near the abbey and frightened everyone near it.

1180 - Kii province, Japan: A term equivalent to our "flying saucer" was actually used by the Japanese approximately 700 years before it came into use in the West. Ancient documents describe an unusual shining object seen in the night as a flying "earthenware vessel." The object, which had been heading northeast from a mountain in Kii province, changed its direction and vanished below the horizon, leaving a luminous trail.

1133 - Japan: A large silvery disk is reported to have come close to the ground.

1113 - Wessex, England: A group of churchmen from Laon in France were going from town to town in Wessex, bearing with them relics of the Virgin Mary, which they used to perform miracles of healing. At the coastal town of Christchuch, they were astonished to see a dragon come out of the sea, 'breathing fire out of its nostrils.'

1078 - England: "In this year appeared the wilde fyr such as no man before remembered: and moreover it did harm in many places."

1034 - Europe: A rare typeset book from 1493 contains what may be the earliest pictorial representation of a UFO. The book, *Liber Chronicarum*, describes a strange fiery sphere, seen in 1034, soaring through the sky in a straight course from south to east and then veering toward the setting sun. The illustration accompanying the account shows a cigar-shaped form haloed by flames, sailing through a blue sky over a green, rolling countryside. This may be the first work that actually contains actual illustrations of UFO's.

1027 - Egypt: During August, a number of "stars" were seen to fly over Cairo and the Nile Delta.

1015 - Japan: Two objects were seen 'giving birth' to smaller luminous spheres over Japan.

927 - France: "In the town of Verdun, like the whole eastern part of France, saw fiery armies appearing in the sky. Flodoard's chronicle reports that they flew over eastern Reims on a Sunday morning in March.

919 - Hungary: An object like a flaming torch was seen in the sky, together with spheres, which flew over giving out a brighter light than the stars.

842 - France: Multicolored armies were seen marching in the sky. These sightings of infernal armies were nocturnal.

840 - Lyons, France: As he was coming out of the Cathedral, Agobard, Bishop of Lyons, saw a mob stoning three men and a woman. Apparently, they had been seen descending in an airship, and claimed to be returning to earth after having been kidnapped by "celestial beings who showed them wonders." At the time, France had a law imposing penalties against creatures that travel on aerial ships. The bishop managed to successfully save the lives of these particular four. This strange law was ratified by at least three French kings; King Pepin the Short, Charlemagne, & Louis I.

810 - Aachen, Germany: Alcuin, the secretary and biographer of Charlemagne states in his work that in 810 when he was on his way from Aachen, he saw a large sphere descend like lightning from the sky. It traveled from east to

west and was so bright it made the monarch's horse rear up so that Charlemagne fell and injured himself severely.

796 - England: small globes were seen about the Sun

793 - England: "dragons were seen flying in the air"

776 - Sigiburg Castle, Germany: As the Saxons were laying siege to Charlemagne's castle at Sigiburg, "flying shields" that were reddish in color appeared in the sky and rained down fire on the attacking army.

763 - County Meath, Ireland: While King Domnall Mac Murchada attended the fair at Teltown, ships were seen in the air.

748 - England: "Ships were seen in the air with their men"

747 - China: Huge flame-breathing dragons were reported being seen in skies, accompanied by men in airships.

746 - England: "Dragons were seen in the heavens."

679 - Japan: Cotton-like material about 5 to 6 feet long fell all over Naniwa, former name of Osaka, and drifted by the wind here and there.

674 - England: "In this year a thin and tremulous cloud, a kind of rainbow, appeared at the fourth watch of the night on the fifth day before Easter, proceeding from the east, and turned into the colour of blood."

671 - Japan: From many locations in Japan, a flaming object was seen flying to the north.

664 - Barking, England: At a monastery a great light appeared in the sky at night and shone over nuns who were singing in the burial-ground. They reported that it lifted up, moved to the other side of the monastery, and then ascended into the night sky. Priests said the light surpassed the brightness of day.

650 - India: One night in the hot season, they (Hariswami and his new wife) were laying on the roof of the summer house. The veil on the woman's face slipped off in the night while a demi-god was seated in his car overhead. His gaze suddenly fell upon her. The demi-god lowered the car and placed her asleep within. She was never seen again. (As told by Hariswami, translated from Hindu by J. Platts)

643 - Japan: "Five colored banners and umbrellas shone in the sky, and descending, hung over the Temple to the sound of various music."

642 - Japan: In Autumn, 9th day, 7th month, during the reign of the Empress Toyo-Tokaro-Ikashi-hi-Tarahishi-Hime "a guest star entered the moon." (The Nihongi book two)

640 - Japan: On the 7th day of the second month of Spring, a star entered the moon. (The Nihongi book two)

619 - Japan: A bright object like a human figure was seen over the Gamo River in Central Japan.

584 - France: The Bishop of Tours in France, is perplexed by curious "domes and golden globes that raced across the sky".

***

The Middle Ages saw the usual fireballs, spheres, silver discs, and cigar shaped objects in the sky. Additionally, a number of drum shaped objects, airships, and dragons were seen. Numerous instances recounted airships with personnel aboard. More than once these airships were seen dragging some kind of anchor along the ground, and one of the occupants was asphyxiated while attempting to disentangle it, while another group of them barely escaped a public stoning as per French law. Several accounts spoke of fleets of colorful sky ships attacking one another or the unlucky human armies battling below.

The Classical Period

457 - Brittany, France: a blazing thing like a globe was seen in the sky. Its size was immense, and on its beams hung a ball of fire like a dragon out of whose mouth proceeded two beams, one of which stretched beyond France, and the other reached toward Ireland, and ended in fire, like rays.

398 - Byzantine Empire: "A thing like a burning globe, presenting a sword, shown brilliantly in the sky over the city. It seemed almost to touch the earth from the zenith. Such a thing was never recorded to have been seen before by man."

393 - Rome: Strange lights were seen in the sky in the days of the emperor Theodosius. On a sudden, a bright globe appeared at midnight and shone brilliantly near the daystar, (Venus). This globe shone little less brilliantly than the planet, and little by little, a great number of other glowing orbs drew near the first globe. The spectacle was like a swarm of bees flying around the beekeeper, and the light of these orbs was as if they were dashing violently against each other. They blended together into one awful flame, and bodied forth to the eye as a horrible two-edged sword. The strange globe, which was first seen now appeared like the pommel to a handle, and all the little orbs, fused with the first, shone as brilliantly as the first globe.

334 - Antioch: In the daytime, a star was seen toward the eastern part of the sky, emitting smoke copiously as if from a furnace from the third hour to the fifth hour.

312 - Italy: Constantine and his army all beheld in the heavens a luminous cross. He claimed to have been shown a cross on the Sun as a sign from Christ that he would triumph over Maxentius.

285 - Fayum, Egypt: St. Anthony witnessed a large silver disk resting upon the sand which suddenly vanished like smoke.

150 - Via Campana between Rome and Capua: Hermes, the brother of Pope Pius I, witnessed a 100-foot-long object, multicolored and "shooting out fiery rays". He watched it land in a cloud of dust and saw a "maiden clad in white" exit the craft.

98 CE - Rome: At sunset, a burning shield passed over the sky. It came sparkling from the west and passed over to the east.

~ 90 CE - Patmos, Greece: A man known as "John" writes *the Book of Revelation* attesting to events he witnessed, including many flying objects, and culminating in his being taken to another planet to observe the landing of a truly colossal cube-shaped ship measuring over 2000 km per side.[1]

80 CE - Scotland: When the Roman emperor, Agricola was in Scotland, wondrous flames were seen in the skies over Caledon Wood on many nights, and when the weather was serene, a ship was seen in the air, moving fast.

---

[1] Ken Goudsward, *UFOs In The Bible* p 141

70 CE - Jerusalem: "On the 21st of May... before sunset there appeared in the air over the whole country chariots and armed troops coursing through the clouds and surrounding the cities." - Josephus, from *the Jewish War; Book CXI*, Tacitus, another Roman historian, confirms this sighting.

60 CE Scotland: A 'ship' was seen speeding across the night sky.

~ 35 CE - Damascus, Syria: While traveling, the apostle Paul witnesses a bright light in the sky that leaves him blinded for three days.[2]

~ 30 CE - Jerusalem, Israel: Two disciples of Jesus, both named Mary, witness a man in dazzling white who descends from the sky, accompanied by an earthquake and causing seizures in the cemetery guards.[3]

~ 5 BCE - Bethlehem, Palestine: Three scholars follow a shining flying object from the east until it hovers over Bethlehem.[4]

9 BCE - Kyushu, Japan: Nine moons were seen in the night sky over the community.

12 BCE - Rome: A bright object hovered over Rome for several days, then melted into flashes resembling torches.

---

[2] Ibid. p 149

[3] Ibid. p 175, Matt 28

[4] Ibid. p 5, Matt 2

42 BCE - Rome: "Something like a sort of weapon, or missile, rose with a great noise from the earth and soared into the sky." - From *Prodigia* of Julius Obsequens

48 BCE - Rome: During a civil war, a fire appeared in the air over Caesar's camp and sent thunderbolts falling upon Pompey's camp. Some distance away two "young men" appeared to announce the result of the battle, then suddenly vanished." – Dio Cassius, *Roman History, Book IV*

66 BCE - Rome: "In the consulship of Gnaeus Octavius and Gaius Suetonius a spark was seen to fall from a star and increase in size as it approached the earth. After becoming as large as the moon it diffused a sort of cloudy daylight and then returning to the sky changed into a torch. It was seen by the proconsul Silenus and his suite." – Pliny, *Natural History, Book II*, Ch. 35

73 BCE - Pontus, Asia Minor: While Roman legions were engaged in battle near the Black Sea against King Mithridates a huge flaming object fell between the two armies. It was said to have a shape like a wine jar and was the color of molten silver.

81 BCE - Spoletium: "a gold-colored fireball rolled down to the ground, increased in size; seemed to move off the ground toward the east and was big enough to blot out the sun." – Obsequens, *Prodigiorum*, Ch. 114

85 BCE - Rome: "In the consulship of Lucius Valerius and Caius Marius a burning shield scattering sparks ran across the sky." – Pliny, *Natural History, Book II*, Ch. 34

90 BCE - Rome: In the territory of Spoletium, in Umbria, a globe of fire, of golden color appeared burning in the north with a terrific noise in the sky, then fell, gyrating, to the earth. It then seemed to increase in size, rose from the earth, and ascended into the sky, where it obscured the disc of the sun, with its brilliance. It revolved towards the eastern quadrant of the sky.

99 BCE - Rome: In Tarquinia, there fell things like a flaming torch in different places from the sky. Towards sunset, a round object like a globe, or round or circular shield took its path in the sky, from west to east.

100 BCE - Rome: "a round shield, burning and emitting sparks, ran across the sky from west to east at sunset.

104 BCE - Ameria and Tuder: weapons in the sky rushing together from east and west, those from the west being routed.

122 BCE - Gaul: "In Gaul three suns and three moons were seen." – Obsequens, *Prodigiorum*, Ch. 114

154 BCE - Compsa: "weapons appeared flying in the sky."

163 BCE - Formice: "In the consulship of Tiberius Gracchus and Manius Juventus at Capua the sun was seen by night. At Formice two suns were seen by day. The sky was afire. In Cephallenia a trumpet seemed to sound from the sky. There was a rain of earth. A windstorm demolished houses and laid crops flat in the field. By night an apparent

sun shone at Pisaurum." – Obsequens, *Prodigiorum*, Ch 114

173 BCE - Lanuvium: "a great fleet was said to have been seen in the sky."

212 BCE - Reate: a "huge stone" was seen flying about in the air.

214 BCE - Hadria: "an altar was seen in the sky and about it the forms of men in white clothes." – Julius Obsequens, *Prodigiorum Libellus*, Ch. 66

217 BCE - Faleri: "the sky had seemed to be rent as it were with a great fissure and through the opening a bright light had shone." – Livy, *History, Book XXII*, Ch. 1

218 BCE - Rome: Glowing lamps were seen in the sky at Praeneste, a shield was observed at Arpi and in the Amiterno district, the sky was all on fire, and men in white garments appeared.

222 BCE - Rome: "Also three moons have appeared at once, for instance, in the consulship of Gnaeus Domitius and Gaius Fannius." – Pliny, *Natural History, Book II*, Ch. 32

223 BCE - Rome: "At Ariminium a bright light like the day blazed out at night; in many portions of Italy three moons became visible in the nighttime." – Dio Cassius, *Roman History, Book I*

329 BCE - Persia: Alexander the Great records two great silver shields, spitting fire around the rims in the sky that dove repeatedly at his army as they were attempting a river crossing. The action so panicked his elephants, horses, and men they had to abandon the river crossing until the following day.

332 BCE Tyre, Phoenicia: During the siege of the trade capital of Phoenicia by the Greeks a fleet of flying shields is described as plunged from the sky and crashed upon the city walls.

468 BCE Greece - Daimachos recounts that a globe of fire crossed the sky several times during the 78th
Olympiad.

***

A number of Roman and Greek historians, including Dion Cassius. Pliny the Elder, Titus Livy, Julius Obsequens, Cicero, Anaxagoras, and Homer relate the appearance of strange lights in the sky, glowing shields, flying swords, multiple moons and suns, golden flying spheres. Numerous encounters describe young men or maiden dressed in white. Fleets of flying objects again were seen to engage in battle with other flying armies or with human forces. Several prominent figures were witnesses, including Emperor Theodosius, Constantine, and Alexander the Great.

520 BC - Persia: The Hebrew prophet Zechariah encounters a woman flying in a metallic basket, two “bird women”, and a cylindrical flying object which could destroy houses.

537 BC - Persia: A green skinned humanoid wearing a loose garment over his metallic fitted jumpsuit, appears to the Hebrew prophet Daniel.[5]

584 BC - Persia: The Hebrew prophet Ezekiel is lifted into the sky by a metallic flying object, and suddenly transported a thousand kilometers to Jerusalem. Once there he goes on to describe in great detail the sights and sounds of the workings of the flying craft and its subsequent take-off.[6] Ezekiel actually saw this same UFO sixteen years earlier as well but gave a somewhat garbled and difficult to interpret description.

740 BC - Persia: The prophet Isaiah seems to have experienced a parallel encounter as that of Ezekiel.[7]

842 BC - Bethel, Israel: Elijah the prophet is taken into the sky by a fiery flying “chariot”.[8]

~1000 BC - Mt. Zion, Israel: King David was taken aboard a flying craft and assisted in battle by “thousands” of flying objects.[9]

---

[5] Ken Goudsward, *UFOs In The Bible*, p 47, Dan 10

[6] Ibid. p 77-86

[7] Ibid p 87

[8] Ibid. p 145, 2 Ki 2

[9] Ibid. p 62-67

~ 1080 BC - Israel: Manoah and his wife (whose name is not given but who soon afterwards becomes the mother of Samson, the world's strongest man), are visited by a strange man who rises up into the sky and disappears.[10]

~ 1300 BC - Mt Sinai, Egypt: Moses and the entire Israelite nation witness many encounters with flying objects of various descriptions, both large and small, including a "pillar of fire" that hovered for an extended period of forty years.[11] Numerous deaths and injuries were sustained as a result of contact. On one occasion, seventy-five of the elders were taken up into a large flying craft for a dinner with the visitors.

1450 BC - Bethel, Israel: Jacob witnesses a series of encounters with humanoid beings that can ascend to the sky.[12]

1500 BCE - Egypt: The Palace of Pharaoh Thutmosis III. Circles of fire are said to have hovered over the palace while fishes, winged creatures, and other objects rained down from the sky.

1550 BCE - Canaan: Abraham witnesses a spherical metal flying object, and receives a humanoid visitor who promises him land.

1766 BCE - China: The Emperor Cheng Tang commissions Ki-Kung-shi to construct a flying chariot. After construction the aircraft was tested, reaching the province of Honan. The vessel was later destroyed by imperial edict,

---

[10] Ibid. p 163, Jdg 13

[11] Ibid. p 7, 41-42, 54, 71, Ex 3, 16, 19, 24, 31

[12] Ibid. p 10-15

as the emperor feared the mechanism might fall into the wrong hands.

2000 BCE - Peru's pre-Incan civilization records that "the gods" were from the star system Pleiades. Inca ruins have been found at elevations of up to 13,000 feet, with stones weighing 20,000 tons. Legend tells of spaceships that came from the stars.

2345 BCE - China: The *Hsui-nan-tzu*, a Chinese classic contains a description of "ten suns" appearing in the sky.

~3000 BCE - China: According to the book "*Memories of the Sovereigns and the Kings*" published in the 3rd century AD, in China, in the third millennium BCE before the birth of Huang Ti or of Chi Yu, "sons from the sky" would descend to Earth on a star which was the shape of a saucer.

3534 BCE - India: According to the *Bhagavad Gita*, flying warships burned and destroyed an entire city and its inhabitants, before "returning to the hand of Vishnu".

8000 BCE - Australia: Aborigine records tell of the "dawn beings" from the stars. Australian aboriginal cave drawings depict celestial beings, with antenna and x-ray style drawings. They were very advanced in "aerodynamics". The boomerang is identical to a modern-day aircraft wing. Aborigine means "from the beginning".

10,000 BCE - China: The Dropa, the name given to visitors from Sirius, came down from the clouds with their air gliders.

10,200 BCE - Iraq: The Igigi begin working for the Anunaki sky masters, according to the Sumerian *Atrahasis Epic*. The Sumerians had extended contact with extraterrestrial civilizations according to their texts. These extraterrestrials also interbred and/or genetically manipulated humans and traveled with them to the stars. The kings were taken to the stars by the extraterrestrials. Their astronomy was highly developed, and they used the zodiac signs to determine earth's place in the galaxy. Some Sumerian documents appear to mention extraterrestrials from Mars, the star system Pleiades, the star Sirius, and the galactic core. These early stories are reflected in biblical texts — Genesis 6 speaks of half breed Nephilim born with Elohim DNA, the Book Of Enoch parallels the star voyages of the kings. The book of Job tells of the migration from the galactic core.

22,238 BCE - Mesoamerica: "Matlactli Atl", the first era of the Mesoamerican Long Count Calendar begins, founded by giants who came to earth from elsewhere.

45,000 BCE - China: Rock carvings of round UFO-like objects have been found in China's Hunan province. The depictions date back to the age of the Neanderthals.

47,400 BCE - Sumer: King En-men-dur-ana was taken up into the sky, according to *the Sumerian king list*.

270,000 BCE - Sumer: *Sumerian king list* starts here with god-kings reigning in the sky.

***

As we move beyond the classical period, we notice a reduction in records. The remaining encounters seem to be less frequent in time as other records are lost. However, the most memorable and important ones remain imprinted in even the sparsest histories, the vimanas of 3rd century BC, and earlier, and their battles and amazing myths surrounding them are a living memory in India. Along with the blueprints as to how to build them and operate them are recorded for all time. The pattern shifts to those of close encounters of the third and fourth kind. As our focus shifts to the entities, they take on more definition: green men, bird-women, giants, dawn beings, and gods come into focus as humanity struggles to comprehend and give meaning to that which does not fit into their frame of reference. Those who are more powerful become gods, elements not explainable become magic or miracles and religions are formed to explain the unexplainable. Pillars of fire, fiery circles, balls of light and discs come forward in time to remain as elements that are sighted to this day.

Summary

For as far back as humans can remember, they have been witnessing similar strange objects in the sky, often accompanied, inhabited, or piloted by strange humanoid creatures who differ in some respect from the witnesses and the general populace. The observational evidence remains remarkably consistent, despite massive changes in the culture, philosophy, and technology of the observers, our own ancestors across a timescale as vast as our own existence. As a phenomenon, UFOs are stable. Whatever we are seeing, we keep seeing the same things. Surely this means something. Surely this indicates something real.

Conclusion

UFO'S - A RIDDLE WRAPPED IN A MYSTERY INSIDE AN ENIGMA

It's a simple fact that UFO's have been visiting the earth for thousands, perhaps millions of years. Ancient texts report them, the Bible speaks of them, cave and rock pictographs record their presence throughout time, and yet, we know not who or what they are, nor their purpose for being here. Ancient cultures, when faced with things they didn't understand, created myths about them to explain their existence. We do the same things as our ancestors, just with bigger words and more tech. Fiction writers have made fortunes fabricating stories about the origins and purpose of these flying objects while borrowing greatly from biblical and Sumerian texts with no visible proof to back them up. But they don't need proof because they publish as fiction... someone should clue in the thousands who take their words as gospel.

So, if UFOs are here, where have they come from? Or perhaps the question should be *when* have they come from. Some of the evidence appears to point to the future. We have already examined the rash of sightings in 1897 all across the midwest and pacific coast. The 1897 sightings all seem to agree that the craft in question was a sort of steam-punk affair. In each case, a similar craft was described – a craft that strongly resembled a dirigible or blimp. Twelve years earlier, the French army had developed successful dirigible technology, but made only a few test flights locally in France and was not capable of long-distance journeys. The historical technological equivalent of the airships of the 1897 sightings did not exist until well into the 1920s. Is it possible that the 1897 airships had come back in time from a near-future where dirigibles were available? As incredible as it sounds, other UFO encounters seem to suggest similar time-travelling scenarios. For the best example, we ourselves must make a temporal jump to the modern age.

In December of 1980 a UFO landed in Rendlesham forest in Great Britain close to two air bases. One of the solders sent out to investigate was Jim Penniston. He described the object that landed as similar to a large drone, and it was covered with markings similar to hieroglyphics. He ran his hand over the drone and was downloaded with a great deal on information but didn't realize it at the time. When he got back to his vehicle, he took out his notebook and wrote down pages of 1's and zero's. Making no sense to him he forgot all about it until decades later he showed it to a friend who recognized it as binary code. When translated, it said in part, "...Exploration of humanity continuous for planetary advance, eyes of your eyes – origin year 8100." In a way this is encouraging because it infers we or our descendants are still here far into the future, for this clearly suggests the craft was a time traveler. The question still is the elephant in the room as to who has been observing us since the beginning of time.

We have gathered ponderous examples of UFO sightings throughout time, and it's very clear whatever they are, they're real. Who or what controls them or their purpose is still anyone's guess, and yet hints have been left across the globe for us to decipher if and when we can figure them out. The Nazca Lines must mean something, they can't just be cosmic graffiti. The Mayan ancient astronaut on the tomb cover was not a random carving, it represented something real, and crop circles created in short amounts of time depicting intricate patterns are not just some alien etch-a-sketch drawings. Most of them have meanings if only we could decipher them.

We send rockets out into space searching for life as we know it, ignoring the fact that it's been circling the planet for eons. In essence, looking for life in all the wrong places and ignoring what's right above our heads. A common problem we humans all have is trying to make hard what are simple truths. Are there UFO's? Of course. Are there aliens/non terrestrials in them? Most probably some of them. Are they here to enslave us? If they are, they're taking their own sweet time in doing so. What are they waiting for to contact us? Most probably waiting for us to stop making up fiction about them and take seriously the messages they are sending us… waiting for us to grow up.

About the Authors

Barbara DeLong is an internationally known radio podcast host, author, artist, lecturer, ordained minister, and documentarian.

- The Cosmic Deck of Initiation – this is a spiritual deck of hand painted mandala cards, which she painted, to be used for private divination and spiritual growth.
- "Whispers of Spiritual Wisdom"
- 2011 Megalithomania conference documentary "Secrets of the Stones" - writer, narrator, co-producer with her late husband Patrick Cooke.
- Her radio podcast, Night-Light Radio is intended to be just that in a time when many are awakening to the gifts and talents that they carry within. Her interviews with authors and gifted individuals help others to gain insight into themselves as well as the reality in which we dwell. She provides a platform for many to share the truths they have uncovered and the insights that can change our perception of the world in which we live.
- Her website, Barbaradelong.com, is a teaching site combining personal information and a plethora of spiritual material.

Ken Goudsward is a systems analyst with expertise in industrial robotics, software engineering, and data design. He enjoys applying these skills to ancient Hebrew and Sumerian documents, and the UFO phenomenon.

Other Books by Ken Goudsward:
- Fermi's Paradox Is Bullshit
- UFOs In The Bible
- Magic In The Bible
- The Enuma Elish; the Original Text With Brief Commentary
- The Atrahasis Epic

Novels by Ken Goudsward:
- Symphony Of Destruction
- Munchausen By Proxy For Fun And Profit

Printed in Great Britain
by Amazon

30100020R10066